Merry Christmas
to
Dad and Patty
1979

A LEAF FROM FRENCH EDDY

BEN HUR LAMPMAN

A LEAF FROM FRENCH EDDY

A Collection of Essays on Fish, Anglers & Fishermen

Illustrated by Heather Preston

Published in San Francisco by
HARPER & ROW, PUBLISHERS
New York, Hagerstown, San Francisco, London

To all men who seek to fathom the mystery
and preserve the beauty created by
sweet waters flowing towards the sea

FIRST HARPER & ROW EDITION PUBLISHED IN 1979.

Designed by Jim Mennick

Library of Congress Cataloging in Publication Data
Lampman, Ben Hur, 1886-1954
A LEAF FROM FRENCH EDDY.
First published in 1965 by the Touchstone Press, Portland, Or., as v. 1 of the author's The Lampman papers.
1. Fishing. I. Title.
SH441.L28 1979   799.1'2'08   78–15836
ISBN 0–06–250500–9

79 80 81 82 83   10 9 8 7 6 5 4 3 2 1

CONTENTS

INTRODUCTION

ANY COLLECTION of Ben Hur Lampman's fishing essays published in the West as a memorial to him should properly begin by acknowledging his origins in the flatlands of North Dakota and the lake country of Wisconsin where he caught his first fish. Early in life, however, he married a vibrant, adventuresome school teacher from upstate New York and together they traveled West into the mountainous grandeur of Oregon where he started his career as a fisherman-printer-writer.

*   *

They settled on the banks of the Rogue River and he printed a weekly newspaper called *The Gold Hill News.* Here, from 1912 to 1916, the lyric Lampman prose first attracted attention and the natives coined a name for him: The Oracle of Gold Hill. Then his competence as a writer took him to Portland where he specialized in polished editorials and nature essays for a daily newspaper. Two of his short stories won O. Henry memorial prizes and critics compared the literary charm of his *The Coming of the Pond Fishes* with Izaak Walton's *The Compleat Angler.*

As a fisherman I found the privilege of searching The Lampman Papers and selecting these essays a pleasant recreation. My esteem for Mr. Lampman grew with each discovery. His tremendous powers of observation, his good-natured appreciation of the various species of fish, and his astonishing exuberance will surely lead some fishermen to refer to him as the American Izaak Walton.

In these pages you will find the vintage prose, the humor and the sentiments which prompt many men to salute Ben Hur Lampman once or more each season with a glass or cup of spirits beside the very waters he fished and wrote about with remarkable luck. Moreover, if you are one of those who have been soothed by the music of rivers and the magic of lakes, one of those who have a reverence for the fish trees and wild life such waters sustain, this will be a *special* book for you. Parts of it are mysteriously haunting . . . inspired phrases and mellow insights such as Coleridge had in mind when he observed that musical writing, with true rhythm and melody in the words, usually possesses something deep and good in the meaning too.

V.S. HIDY

On the Metolius,
Above Wizard Falls

A LEAF FROM FRENCH EDDY

I. DISCOVERY

A Kind of Pagan Sorcery More Rewarding Than the Catch

A LEAF FROM FRENCH EDDY

A golden-veined leaf of scarlet, enclosed in a letter, is said by the writer of the note to be "part of a day's catch at French eddy." And the letter asks if one ever has been to French eddy, where the leaf was picked. Yes, often, but not often enough. It is said that we tire soon of all things that grow commonplace to us, and in tiring grow indifferent to their virtues, as children weary of playthings to which they are long accustomed. But it is not to be imagined that one would tire soon, or at all, of that broad and secret pool, with the current racing beyond it, which lies cupped in the hand of the hills. Of itself the eddy is sovereign for weariness. And part of the catch at French eddy always is more than trout.

*   *

Long and long ago, when the mail was fetched up the river by boat, through the green swift reaches and over the shallows of sun and shadow, French eddy—so they say—was the upper terminal of the service. This margin, where the water ouzels come to beg dole of fishermen, has long been familiar to people, and once it was of truly utilitarian importance. The eddy had an official status in those times. Now it is only a fishing hole on the excellent river that creates it. But to a great number of people, when they fall to thinking of rivers —which is one of our devices for enumerating the days that have mattered—this loitering of waters where the trout assemble must symbolize their river, their own especial river. For when you think of rivers, there is one river that runs before all. And that sort of spell was cast, long ago, when the river carved its channel, at French eddy.

*   *

"There is," said the letter, "a ghost of a forest across the stream. The mists lift from the top of Euchre mountain, and the hills are as clean as a window newly washed." Yes, it would be like that, on a fall day between rains The hills are quite breathlessly cleansed. In their breathless quietude the hills almost are exclamatory. But have ever you been at French eddy when the hills send tribute to the river, by their thousand minor watercourses that are affluents of the great stream, and the haste of the river is jeweled with dancing rain, and the driftwood begins its final pilgrimage—down and down to the sea? Then is a very good time for fishing at French eddy, and to taste rain on one's lips, and to be driven back, and back, by the rising river, while the trout are elate and hungry. The eddy is famous in those parts for the steelhead trout that swing valiantly in from the current, on such a day, to explore the gravel they knew in infancy.

*   *

Of course, and surely, one has been to French eddy, and often—but not often enough. There is ever something more in the catch, at French eddy, than the trout that come to the creel, or the steelhead that are beached gleamingly in the rain. An artistry touched these secret swift fishes, and lingered over their modeling, the hue of their flanks. It was, it must have been, akin to that instruction which taught the water ouzel how to walk upon the silt, with the stream flowing round and over. And in the half of a minute the hill, that dark pagan, with mists at his head, will speak with a voice, and the words will be wisdom. For manifestly the hill has something in thought that requires to be said. Have ever we been to French eddy? Why, surely. But send no scarlet leaf from that place to us, until we may go again.

THIS FISHING!

It is remembered as clearly in every essential detail as though it had been yesterday. Over the planks of

Poskin's dam, and these were painted a dull green with water mosses, the stream trickled thinly. There were willows, quite as a matter of course, and the bank was lush with the tenderest of clover, cropped close by cattle. And where the water fell into the pool, there was carried, down and down, an interminable outpouring of false pearls that rose streamingly to the surface and fizzed into nothingness. Save for this the pool was forbiddingly dark and mysterious, yet it exercised a spell not all unpleasing. It held a promise, it extended an expectancy, that I have since remarked in many waters. And somebody said, with the least trace of mature impatience, sharply, urgently:

"Pull him in! Land sakes! You got a bite!"

I pulled. Upward along the line, through my fingers, and thence to every dancing nerve, tingled the message of my captive, struggling in the dark water beneath Poskin's dam. And my heart sang to his strugglings and magnified his might. Out of mystery he rose, gnomish of aspect and mildly blue of eye, with every barbel waving, and pectoral spines fiercely set, that singular catfish we called bullhead—seven tremendous inches of him. He shone on the clover as ebony would, and leviathan seemed not more vast to the ancient father who fleshed the first harpoon. I was seven and this my maiden fish.

*   *

I hold it to be a goodly heritage that wherever water is found, salt or fresh, land-girt or sweetly flowing, there fish are to be had in nearly every instance. Nor can

there be a loneliness more inconsolable than that of
some desolate lake which, heavily burdened with
minerals, may not be host to fishes, but lies barren and
lamenting, with never a scaled flank to flash above it,
and never a fin to cruise casually amid its secret places.
To harbor fish is the proper heritage of every water,
and foremost among the rights of man, all landed
proprietors to the contrary, with a plague on placards of
trespass, is the right to wet a line and take a fish.

* *

It is pleasant to observe that the eldest and most
democratic of all fraternities is that of the fishermen,
wherein membership is shared by the veriest aboriginal
and the most cultured of cosmopolites. These speak a
kindred language and are never at loss to comprehend
one another when the theme is fishing. What is this
fishing?

One has no difficulty in distinguishing mere anglers
from your true fisherman. Though it is possible for the
individual to be both angler and fisherman, or almost, it
is a phenomenon of great infrequency for any fisherman
to be an angler or to wish to become one. The
fisherman is artlessly gratified by the simpler expressions
of the urge to fish. He will fish, doggedly, happily, with
the aptness of the perfect convert, in waters where a
strike is extremely improbable, and at seasons when
every natural sign is against him. He will fish when
thunders are above, and lightnings streak the sky. He
will fish with the sleet in his face and the wind chilling
him to the marrow. He will fish with a knotted cord of

cotton and the crudest of hooks. It is true that the finer
gear of the craft, superlative, beautiful, masterly, is very
dear to him—but the urge to fish is dearer. He fishes
because he must fish.

* *

So, as I have said, it began for me with the capture
of a catfish—the most personable and handsome catfish
—in the black pool below Poskin's dam. I drew from
the earliest water something more than a catfish—a
charmed creature, weaving spells. If I required his life
of him, he in his turn exacted a tribute that has not
wavered. The sorcery of him has led me to my armpits
in frigid mountain water, of which I derived twinges
that linger; and to shores of summer where the sun
flayed me, face and arm—and shall lead again. I, too,
am well content.

* *

I would pass rapidly on, for the sin of fishermen is
that of tedium, to the adventure of the floating island,
which befell a few years later. The lake is in Wisconsin,
and for all I know to the contrary the selfsame islands
cruise it yet. They were masses of treacherous bogland,
half peat, half deeply rooted waterplants thriving in
their own decay, and they floated heavily over the lake
and the wind's will, now here, now miles away. Only
boys, with the casual bravado of their kind, fished from
the treacherous vantage of these wanderers.

Each island reared a numerous brood of black frogs,
and it followed that each island was ringed with
watchful eyes. That incautious frog who quitted the

quaking mass, though ever so briefly, was seen no more by his fellows. In a gleam and a swirl the bass or pickerel struck, and where the swimmer had been there was only a momentary eddy with a bubble whirling on its rim. Of boats we had none to command, but when an island came within tempting distance of the mainland we pushed out on logs and gained it, and at sunset were known to walk through town with such strings of mighty fish, and mostly of bass, as brought the loungers to attention. But these were our islands and we did not tell. So long ago and far away.

*   *

And three of us voyaged one day not to a single island only, but to all three of them, for the weather was auspicious and the log extraordinarily obedient. It was so that the forebears put out from shore. We had reversed the record and were again at the beginning of things. Here and there, on the two islands first visited, and from the log in mid-lake, we took fish—bass with the scent of sweet herbes rising from their fat sides, lean, savage pickerel mottled and barred, and that fish called the wall-eyed pike, which when taken from a certain bottom is golden as a coin. Yet the catch had been but a fair one when we moored the log insecurely to the third island and tossed our frogs beside its rushes.

The island lay near the mouth of a river and the swing of the waning current played with it musingly. Deep and deeper sank my frog, till white stomach was lost to view in green shadow, and I began—for it was our custom to kill this bait before we used it—that jerking motion of the 5-cent cane, which caused the luckless batrachian to seem to swim. There was a reluctance manifest. The line drew slowly outward and downward, and, lacking the refinement of a reel, I moved the tip toward the surface and thrust it under, and still under, until my eager wrist was in the water. And I struck.

*   *

A fisherman would know, and an angler might know —though I doubt many anglers have fished after that fashion. The vibrant, furious berserk rage of him! The whiteness of his flanks, far down, far down. The rush that sent him twisting into the June sunshine. The dread that swept me, lest he should be lost. And at long last, by the clemency of those fates that watch over fishermen, and give particular heed to boys, the drawing forth of a great pike or pickerel that weighed unbelievable pounds, and that was borne home between two of us on a stout stick as becomes a mighty fish who has fought the good fight and can no more.

Does pride know a summit loftier than this? Or fullness of heart a deeper, more pervasive content? Why, sir, I assure you that even an angler might have been dislodged from his studied nonchalance by the taking of that magnificent specimen of its species.

*   *

The time came for the catching of my first trout, and this is always a memorable experience. For the trout, of whatever kind, is not appraised for weight alone, but for those finer values which are found in fluent outline, in grace, and glow and all of beauty's attributes. He who catches a trout has in the rough, mortal hand of him one of nature's poems, a creature of a comeliness so rare, so strange, so patrician, as to touch the heart of the captor with pity and with praise. And they who take tarpon, I dare say, those vast and valorous herrings that are silver as a shield, do not take with their tarpon that certain something which every fisherman takes with his trout, though the fish be no longer than a stretched finger. This trout of mine, this first trout, was taken in the creek we knew as Four-Mile.

*   *

Thickets of hazel and sumac pressed close to Four-Mile, and willows waded lithely into its sweet current, and in all it was such a stream as is hard to come at, and such a one as you might cross almost at a stride. In that creek, I remember, I first saw the miller's thumb, that universal ugliness, that finned belly, which is the bane of bait fishermen. He came squattering over the bright sand, as he were come from the moon, strange, lunar, outlandish. I drew the grasshopper from his gullet, and kept the miller's thumb, for fish are fish to a boy. And very stealthily I moved toward that place where Four-Mile made music under a hanging sod. Within the music were trout, many trout, untaught, uncaught, and uncommonly hungry. Ha! He was fast. He was forth. He was mine.

*   *

And thus, by this and by that, and here and there, in one hundred waters, I became an indifferent but incurable fisherman, such as must fish when the wind fares from the wrong quarter, such as yearn from a train toward the merest shimmer of a creek through the first, such as brood hopefully beside pasture ponds, and are guided by an innocent faith which passes understanding.

ALMOST TIME FOR TROUT

There are reasons for this and for that, and we hear much of their openings, but really there is only one season that matters to many men at this time of the year. Looking out of office windows. Driving along in trucks. Handling freight down at the yards. Or walking a beat in the rain. There is one season that is best of all. That, of course, is the trout season which is to open very soon. It is good to live in a land where there is plenty of trout fishing. You never tire of it, and never does the season open without the old tingling, the old response.

People try to explain it, although this is unnecessary, but nobody ever has been quite able to do so, not even Walton. But most fishermen are agreed there is a quality in trout fishing that approaches the ideal. It is like the pursuit and realization of a pleasing dream. The trout is its symbol of abundant reward. It is something like this: We know, of necessity, that we can never have all to which we aspire, and we realize, too, that the dreams of aspiration have a way of fading, and yielding, until they are gone beyond recovery, and we have but memories of them. Is it sad? No. That isn't it. This is the common experience of mankind. We are reconciled to it, or nearly so. Yet men must dream of a time, if it be no more than a single day, when their dreams shall come true, even as they dreamed them. Now the virtue of trout fishing is that it, of all pursuits, rewards the dreamer with realization of his dream. The trout are more beautiful than he remembered them as being, and the day, the scene and the occupation are at harmony. That is why men go trout fishing.

It has often been remarked by trout fishermen that when they are about the affairs of stream and rod, the events of yesterday and the necessities of tomorrow are singularly dwarfed in importance. They seem somehow to lack for real significance. The beauty of stream and forest, the beauty of the fish, the agreeable nature of the employment—these are real. All else appears to be of little moment, and to wear an aspect of trickery, as though men were both betrayed into and by it. It is for this reason that men go trout fishing, vowing that they prefer it to other recreations. Physically weary as they are before the sun is high, the truth is they are resting. They have rediscovered the escape. The stream they fish is running through their hearts to bear away the frets and worries of yesterday and tomorrow. All fishermen will know how it is, though it is uncommonly difficult to explain.

*　　*

If any city dweller could enumerate at this moment the citizens, working and dwelling within a dozen miles of him, whose thoughts are fixed upon the opening of the trout season, he would be astonished at the number of them. And if he might, at the same time, appraise the gentleness and innocence of their reflections, he must be even more astonished by the essential boyishness of their natures. A recreation which sets aside the usual desires, and banishes the common thought of gain and selfishness—as any true recreation should—must be of important benefit to the people that practice it, and therefore to the commonwealth. The state could make no sounder investment than in trout. Such fishing is beneficial to the nature of the citizen. Anything that will persuade a great number of people to think sanely, and decently, and happily, though it be but of a favorite recreation, is of great importance to society.

But no trout fisherman is thinking of this, and small blame to him. He has more important matters to ponder. He must think of his flies and his tackle. He must speculate upon the probable condition of the water. He must recall, and this effortlessly, the very look and laughter of the stream to which he will be going. Mr. Coolidge says that fishing improves the republic, and Mr. Hoover holds the same view. But though we applaud their discernment, we submit that they have told us nothing not already known. There's a stream down toward the coast that should be right, as trout fishermen say, just right, in a day or so.

OPENING DAY

Where shall we go, you say? Let's go back to the place where the tall fern is parted under the first at the brink of the canyon, and the black trail plunges down, with handholds of sapling and root, to white water— down, down to the South Fork. With the salmonberry blooming, and the blue grouse hooting, and somewhere a wild pigeon mourning its heart out. The voice of the South Fork comes up from the canyon till the air pulses with it, and as you go down, down, where the deer have gone, you glimpse the tossed swiftness of the long rapids. Now the last few yards of the trail are steep as a church roof—but here, gray-walled and clamoring, unforgotten, with a hatch dancing above the green swirl by the black rock, here is the South Fork. Do you remember? Let's go back.

*   *

Do you remember? Yonder's the log jam that was many a freshet in making, and the green water lifts without foam as the river slips under the barrier. If trout come out from under the satiny weave of it, they are likely to be large fish, and from much dwelling in shadow are apt to be darkly gleaming. And they will strike where the water lifts—instant and visible and strong. It is a place where the water ouzel sings, as once we heard him; a place where the swifts hunt the little wind of the canyon, for the fly hatch, as once we saw them. It is a place where the mink stares at you, wonderingly, glistening. How far, how very far above, the canyon's brink seems. How small the firs and how foreshortened. The hawk calls as he crosses over. And wild, and fond, and far the place is, and beyond the log jam is the great bar and the long riffle. Let's go back.

*   *

Where shall we go, you say? Let's go back to the place where the paunchy, lithe, shining grandfather of all trout rose thrice, and at the third rise struck smashingly—to leap unbelievably! The reel sings. Not under the trailing branch! Not there! Back to the place where you beached the big trout, bigger even than he had seemed, and the sunshine that fell on the sandbar warmed the rose of his flanks and his cheeks, and the green, and the gold, and the silver and all the glory of him. And plain on the sand is the print of the cougar's great paw. So that one looks at the tangled steepness, up and up to the brink of the canyon—looks and wonders. And here a trout and there a trout, and each of us wet to the armpits, and a sort of feeling that we have come home again. Let's go back.

Do you remember? Well, then, let's go back to the canyon of the South Fork—or someplace—where we used to go. To get so tired from the fishing, but never of fishing, that the very ache of our tiredness is good to feel. Back where we used to go. Let's skirt the black cliff again hazardously—watch out for that rodtip!—and fish once more to the bend and then take time off to make coffee over a driftwood fire. And lie on the sand with a tussock of clover for pillow and from under the brims of our hats watch the high clouds wander over. And lie on the sand and talk, or keep silent, and wonder about how far the car is. And count our trout, maybe, and clean them. It is odd about happiness. The hour glass that measures it is both swift and slow. Do you remember the place where we used to fish? Let's go back.

II. SANCTURY

*Alone with His Secret Thoughts, Golden
Flowers, Kingfishers & Trout*

EVERYONE SHOULD OWN A RIVER

Everyone should possess a river, to have and to hold
for his own; and there is this about a river, that a
thousand may have such rights in its glancing
brightness, the moody green secrecy of its eddies, as
one possesses. Everyone should possess a river, for a
river, well owned, will seem somehow to cleanse its
proprietor, as his river washed the soot and the shame
quite away from small Tom the sweep. And in this
region a river is simply obtained.

So we three went up the river, to share it, Gene and
Tony and I, and the sunlight on the water was such
wonder as no artificer in metals might hope to attain.
There were flights of wild pigeons cast over the river,
the curve and flow of the river, and back in the timber

the pigeons were calling one to another. We had borrowed Mr. Davis's boat. Ho, river! But nobody said that aloud. Ho, river! friend to the fishermen.

*   *

When one owns a river by natural right, as may any, not least of the pleasures of this possession are those that arise out of memory, as a trout will rise, either slowly, bright turning, or flashingly into the morning, to strike at the drifting fly. Sorcerous memory, alchemic, eudemonic, that permits one to touch once more the elusive pattern of yesterday—and, this is strange, in some manner to obtain yesterday more closely, to hold it more dearly, than when yesterday was itself the present. Who owns a river by natural right travels it with memory.

*   *

You friends in far places, who were not with the three of us then, in that today which is yesterday now, you who also have rights in the river, shall know by this information that little is changed on the river since last you experienced it. Little is changed on the river. The gray driftwood below the big bend, it is gone. It was carried away by the turbulent winter water, and the beaches have it now. On the hillside where the loggers lived the shacks have all been dismantled, and the forest is taking the hill again, and the trails are thickly grown with young trees and wild vine, and the vine maple, and fern that is high as your waist. The forest is taking its own again, and one must glance twice to determine that this is the place of the jack salmon pool.

But the snag where you tethered the boat, when the
bright sea-run salmon were striking, has held to its
moorings. Little is changed on the river—for rivers,
though changing, are changeless and constant.

*   *

The selfsame trick of the light on the flow of the
river, the same murmur and laughing, reiterant,
ceaselessly uttered. The selfsame familiar astonishment,
as when the prow swerves round the sweep of the eddy,
and the black rock lifts from the white water and all
the long riffle is dancing. And yonder it was that you
camped, and twilight with bended head came out of
the hills, and your fire thrust redly into the evening
mists. Yonder it was that you camped.

Sudden and swift and brief, the swerve of a flank in
the sunlight, under the drooping maple, and Gene said
prayerfully: "He was all of 14 inches! I tell you, a
regular he-one!" Then Tony held the boat to the
current, in the whispering flow of the river, and the
lure glistened shoreward again, descending there where
that living instancy briefly had risen. He issued like
pliant silver, radiant, out of the shadow, and the rod
curved to the strike. The trout leaped high from the
river, shaking the tackle. But when the net slipped
under, and the fish was lifted, he was no more than
twelve—say ten—and Gene said, with an attempt to
seem casual, "He looked a lot bigger."

*   *

"They are bigger," vowed Tony. "Such fish are
always two inches longer, if not better than that, before

they are caught. It is a very remarkable fact."

On the bar where one November day, with the stream coming up like a mill race, we caught the season's first steelhead, Tony went downstream searching for crawfish. You must know, as you will if you have rights in the river, that when summer is newly come, there is no bait or lure to equal a crawfish that lately has shed its armor, and that hides away, while the new shell hardens, under the rocks and the driftwood. He called to us, above the shouting of the water: "The deer have a crossing here!" And from the margin of the sand, where is an admixture of clay, he brought the track of a fawn in the palm of his hand. He brought it carefully, the sign of the fawn.

* *

"It's a fawn track," Tony explained. "The fawn came down with its mother." He turned to look at the haste of the river. "I wonder," he said, "if that fawn's old lady really crossed over there with her fawn. It's the littlest fawn track ever I saw."

* *

We three considered the fawn track. It might have been made on the brink of the river by the goat-foot himself, the river-god Pan, when he was a little-small fellow, with melodies vexing him sweetly, formless, insistent. It was only a fawn track. But the near and listening forest became on this moment suddenly peopled, watchful, alert, and yet drowsy. A pigeon called in the fir-top. The pagans, heaven love them, they were the most reasonable of all unreasonable beings. Who shall abandon wonder? And what remains to him then? The print of the fawn's cleft hoof fell to the verge of the river, and a newt, orange-bellied, turned to observe this.

Of such small matters, soon sped, is a day on the river comprised. The trout? Enough trout were taken to warrant the voyage. But as somebody said about trout, and it must have been Master Walton, it isn't the trout that are first in this fishing. He owned several rivers by natural right, as all men should own at least one.

*   *

Toward evening we dropped down the river again, Gene and Tony and I, and the heron rose hoarsely out the shallows into the eye of the sun, and we were tired, and all was as it should be. We tied up the boat and went home, relinquishing but yet possessing the river. It is a considerable comfort to know that the river will be there when we return. Sir, in this inconstant, shifting vagary that constitutes the usual way of life, it is a considerable comfort to realize that the river will always be there.

Everyone ought to possess a river by natural right.

ASPECTS OF THE ANGLING COMPLEX

In a world too often open to criticism, for this reason or that, it has been providentially arranged that anglers never should grow up. This in itself is compensation for many a trouble and great variety of disappointments.

For, having tasted the freshness of a morning in mid-April, along some stream where leaps at least an occasional trout, what angler is not the younger for this? An eagerness that causes his fingers to fumble with line and leader, that dispatches a pleasing nervousness from head to heel, is the earnest of that zest for living which is lost, or, mostly, at the crossroads of boyhood and maturity by all save anglers and other excellent fellows. In fine, this angler of whom one speaks is in that moment and that vicinage no longer the man he was but yesterday. The frothy current at his feet may flow, for all that you may say, from that same spring the Spaniard sought at the eventual forfeit of his life. The secret is well worth having.

*   *

You must comprehend that such analytical flights of fancy as this in which we have indulged ourselves, and which hover very near to the fact, may not be orally indulged when anglers are present, and more particularly when tackle is out. For your true angler is a man of puzzled reticences who would be as embarrassed so to discuss his pastime as another would be to prate of a charming wife, or of an equally personable maiden whose hand he seeks. There is resident in the Waltonian, save when he is alone with his secret thoughts, a marked disinclination to confess that he has seen a passing cloud mirrored in the river, and that so small an experience as this must remain in his memory until he crosses Jordan water, with a final thought for the fishes that must frequent its clouded flow. Do not, therefore, speak to him of aught save trout and tackle, or of other fish, as the case may be, if you would not be rebuked by a look or possibly an explosive impatience. For he has convinced himself, or so he likes to pretend, that he angles for fish.

*   *

Now, angling for the silver-flanked trout is well enough, in its way; indeed, it is such angling as can have no superior, whether in salt water or fresh. But the angler dissembles somewhat when he gives it as his opinion that he, and others of his fraternity, are catching trout and nothing else, unless it be a whitefish or so, or possibly a chub. This conclusion is not susceptible of serious argument when it is agreed that these same trout, tamed and held in an ugly pool of angular concrete, would not and could not arouse the enthusiasm of anglers, or kindle their eyes with unaccustomed brightness. It is true that an angler might deign to angle in such a pool as is described, but his heart would not be there, and a cynic shadow would rest upon his countenance. He would do so, if, indeed he yielded, for the sufficient reason that no wilder water was near at hand or lawfully available. You must remember that in this frequent praise of Isaak Walton, whose memory is green as a willow in Devon—and properly so—we have more or less forgotten another angler, who was Simon called Simple. Ah, there was the personification of the inward angler, or the driven fisherman! Of the fisherman who must fish! Of perennial and patient optimism! But we set out to prove that sans the setting the delights of angling would be negligible and antic. And this, it now appears, requires no further demonstration.

For they who angle for silver-flanked trout, and who will penetrate the blessed wilderness this day, shall catch the golden mimulus where it grows in the cold clay of the river bank, and the picket-fence rattle of the belted kingfisher flashing by, and an odor of fern, and the roar and shouting of waters, and laughter, and that far sound that is the wraith of a sound—the reiterant bell-like music of silence in the forest. True, if fortune favors them they will catch fish also, and lose fish, too, and boast mightily of their adventuring and their cleverness. But the weight of the laden creel at evening is not the worth of the outing, and well they know it. Nevertheless, be chary of how you suggest these other matters to them, for they are pleased to think they are practical fellows, and sinewy sportsmen, as red-blooded as the hero of a book by Zane Grey. If they turn upon you with profanity, please remember at least that you were forwarned. Good fishing!

WHEN WALTON FISHED THE DOVE

It is now the opening day of the trout fishing season, and many the angler has been up before dawn, and off and away under the stars to his stream, while the name of that water was a sort of music in his thought. Dairy creek. Rock creek. Or the Nehalem. Drift creek.

Schooner creek. Or the bright twisting of the Siletz. The two Nestuccas, Beaver creek, Canyon creek. The Calapooya. Or the long dancing reaches of the upper Willamette. The names of their streams fled like silver water through their reflections, and they saw, as they hastened, the black rocks that are garmented with moss midway of the foam and the laughter. For the name of a stream will become, to men that go fishing, as something possessed and living, that stirs about in their hearts and whispers over and over.

* *

On such a morning as this, when Derbyshire was waking to April, the good Master Walton went down to his river, which he had called "that delicate river," the Dove. There were trout flies in his dingy hat, and lively gentles in a wooden box in his pocket, and in his hand the long and well-beloved English trouting rod was waggling, and sundry birds were singing to him from the hedgerows. At first glimpse of the Dove, where it sparkled and sang to him through the trees, almost there was a catch in his throat and a glad wetness in his eyes, for the river, the morning, the birds, the dear brightness of it all, and to be going a-fishing again. "God never did make," quoth he, "a more calm, quiet, innocent recreation than angling." And Master Walton caused the tip of his trouting rod to whistle in the bright, damp breeze, and in such haste was he then, and of such eagerness, that almost he loitered to have the fine flavor of anticipation. But presently he cast a dun-fly in the pool by the willows, and a trout rose swirlingly to strike. On such a morning as this, when Derbyshire was rousing to April, all of three centuries since.

*   *

Aye, marry, sirs—that was an excellent fish, indeed, though it was taken all of three centuries ago. Its tail was thrust out of the basket, wherein its rounded snout rested against the green grasses, and now and again Master Walton peered at his fish, as to make sure it was there, and he not mistaken about having taken it properly from the willow pool with a dun-fly. Men change very little in three centuries, though nations themselves disappear, but fishermen change not at all.

THE THREE PRINCIPAL SPECIES OF FISHERMEN

As for me, I have no patience with trolling, and though I consider fly fishing to be the poetry of angling, I find the most substantial prose of this consoling diversion to be in bait fishing. It is true that the troller often catches the larger fish, and that the compensations of a changing scenery and a superior deftness remain to the fly fisherman; but for the more solid satisfaction of fishing I greatly prefer the gentle eddy and the waiting rod. There is a captain of police who esteems himself a fly fisherman of parts, and whose inclination toward that sort of angling has even progressed so far that he captures luckless bugs and ephemera along the water courses, and, bearing these home with him, contrives very passable imitations thereof in wool, and silk, and the feathers of orient fowl, as the jungle cock. Such he swears by, and mightily, for it is true that they will entice fish, quite as a scrap of red flannel, impaled on a hook, will bring a hungry trout flashing to the surface.

But I regard him as a genial fellow gone somewhat astray, and as one who has befooled himself that there is merit in deceit. Time was when he cast away hundreds of pounds of salmon eggs, which are a favorite bait in our northwestern streams, with the best of them, ere he was converted to that super-refinement which lifts its lip in scorn of all save the fly, and the dry fly at that. It is something to see nowadays the blended anguish and horror that enter his eyes at the merest mention of bait fishing. He winces as at physical pain. But, sirs, he has lost forever the very amiable odor of driftwood fires in a slow rain, which it is the habit of bait fishermen to kindle while they await the strike. And if he would but read Walton, whose name he reveres, he would discover that the patron saint of anglers and honest men—for they are one—believed as implicitly in baits of sundry sorts as he did in the virtues of those false gauds that are styled flies. My friend has, or so I believe, so hedged himself about with dogma, with form and ceremony, that he has quite lost the true flavor of his favorite sport, and is as inextricably snarled in his own delusions as a hook in a tangled creel.

*   *

Your troller squats in a boat, excessively
uncomfortable, continually beset and plagued by a
desire that the craft proceed either faster or more
slowly. It is ordained that he shall never, or seldom, be
content with the speed at which he travels, even as it is
ordered that he shall alternate between reeling in his
lure to disentangle such debris as water weeds, and
halting the boat to recover the spinner from some
lurking and obdurate snag. The stress upon his line is
now greater than it should be, now less, and always he
is fretted by the dark suspicion that the blade of the
lure is not turning and twinkling as it should. When he
has hooked his fish he runs aground or is swept far
down stream by the current, and when he has not
hooked his fish he runs aground anyway. Coupled with
this, there is a perversity of the red gods which decrees
that the leader often shall break or the hook work free
as he brings his captive to gaff or the net. He has been
known to fall in, always ungracefully, and to emerge
wetter than any salmon that ever swam the tides. His
is, indeed, a melancholy and vexatious pastime, fraught
with vicissitudes and cares. Even granting that it is
better than no fishing, still it is relatively a thankless
and sorrowful pursuit.

*   *

Angling is, or should be, essentially a philosophic and
reflective engagement, rewarding the practitioner not
only with trouts, but with a gentler and more matured
comprehension of life itself. No sort of form or whim

of angling, of which I am aware, is as admirable to this end as bait fishing. I have the honor of acquaintance with a fisherman whose culture has so far progressed that, having equipped himself with various fatal deceits and provenders, gadgets and thingumbobs and barbs, and having reached the stream with a heart resolute and bold, does no more than recline upon the clover and spy out the affairs of the trout. He spends hours in this occupation, and though his creel is empty at sunset, his heart is full. In more than a manner of speaking he is the perfected angler, putting us all to shame, since his philosophy, his acceptance of life, has reached that station whence it looks calmly down upon the lust of fishing as some soul in Nirvana. But for his imperfect fellows, who are rent between primitive urges and swami-like trances, bait fishing must continue to answer both their lower and their higher needs.

Not only has the bait fisherman time and plenty for amiable conversations, if he is companioned—the which is half of fishing—but he has leisure, if soul alone, for communion with river bank, and cloud, and tree, and the bright westward breeze. He has time, too, for the brewing of coffee, and he knows—as never troller or fly fisherman can truly know—the ancient and valid hunger for wood smoke. For though it may fill his eyes with tears, nevertheless the sharp tang of it, the keen, wet savor of it—wood smoke being at its best on a day of rain—permeate him with a strange and elder contentment. The line twitches in the sedately swirling water. A sapphire that is a kingfisher gleams by while far out in midstream there is upreared a massive salmon falling heavily. Oh, heart too full of happiness. Oh, eyes that see beyond the gates of dream.

*   *

Oftentimes the bait fisherman catches fish, though, truth to tell, oftentimes he does not. His eddy is shattered by the strike, the leap, the long and lusty run —or it remains mysteriously unvexed of incident. But more often than any other kind of fishermen those who fish with bait are heard to say that, after all, it doesn't matter. Now the purpose of fishing, the philosophic purpose, is to teach that it does not matter—that nothing matters save contentment, and that contentment is far easier to bring to creel than any fish. It is true that the lesson grows vague or is lost, between fishings, but to hold and to have the meaning of it for so little while as a day is a great gain to us.

Should you see a man diligent in bait fishing, regard him well. He is a dependable fellow, warm of heart and hand, who will open his tackle box to you or share his coffee. Sit beside him and talk a while.

A FEW FISH STORIES

Our inquiring reporter, who has an exceptional flair for the discovery and extraction of amazing true stories from real life—the kind that make you shake your head dazedly and exclaim, "Indeed, truth is stranger than fiction!"—has filed the following authenticated reports of actual occurrences and adventures variously experienced on the opening day of the trout season. In each instance the facts have been carefully checked and verified by a committee of fellow fishermen, all of whom are among the present raconteurs. Since comment would naturally be superfluous this newspaper refrains from it, and presents the local, national and international records hereinafter established:

*　　*

Tennyson Brooks spent the opening day on the upper reaches of Otter creek. It will be remembered by many fishermen that this portion of the stream, although famous for its fighting cutthroat trout, has in other years been barred to anglers by Old Bill Trivett, who was reputed to enforce his edict with a shotgun. On this occasion, however, Mr. Trivett met Mr. Brooks just as the latter was half-way through the barbed-wire fence, and cordially invited him to come along in. "Make yourself right to home," said Mr. Trivett, "and don't pay no attention to them trespass notices." Thereafter, the genial old gentleman escorted Mr. Brooks to several of the better holes.

Using a No. 10 fly, an iron blue dun, Oscar Squinch, the popular hardware salesman, snagged into a monster trout at the foot of the Zilditch riffle late in the afternoon. Mr. Squinch likes to give a fish the sporting chance, and his leader was but of two-pound weight. At the first rush, in that fast water, the trout—which seemed as large as a salmon—ripped off 30 yards of line. It was then that Mr. Squinch sat down in the middle of the riffle. When he got up, the trout was still on. He was prepared to make affidavit that this trout was as long as his arm. After a terrific struggle, lasting more than half an hour, when angler and trout were equally exhausted, the enormous fish made one last desperate dash—but the leader did not part, the hook did not break, and the reel did not fall off. Mr. Squinch landed the big fellow. It proved to weigh three and one-quarter pounds more than he thought it would.

*   *

J Addison Pabst fished the south fork of the Pootle from sunrise to sundown. He reports the water as being slightly discolored and the trout reluctant to take his lures, although he employed, at appropriate intervals, dry fly, wet fly, spinner, salmon egg and angleworm while fishing the stream with that skillful thoroughness for which he is celebrated. Yet when he took down his rod, preparatory to leaving the river, he had but seven minor trout to show for a day's angling. By curious coincidence, a small, tatter-clad boy, barefooted and freckled, of course, the son of a neighboring farmer, came along at that moment. The boy had a willow for his rod, a few yards of knotted cotton-twine for his line, and a three-for-a-penny hook. He, too, had been fishing the Pootle since shortly after dawn. The little urchin had no fish whatsoever.

HEATHER PRESTON

III. SUSPENSE

Triumph & Disaster, a Silver Mystery, a
Straying Wind & Other Works of Art

HOW HE FISHED THE WEST FORK

Yes, indeed—said the Old Copy Reader—you may
number me among those pagan celebrants, sometimes
called anglers, who fittingly observed the opening of the
trout season. May I tell you in confidence that when I
had finished opening it, that long and eagerly
anticipated day resembled—as you might say figuratively
—a sardine can that has been assaulted with a cleaver?
A little ragged around the edges, no doubt, but
indisputably opened. The art of angling, so I have read
in books, instructs one in philosophy. I suppose it must,
because long ago I became truly philosophic about my
opening days.

*　　*

Ah, thank you—sighed the Old Copy Reader
comfortably—I left my cigarettes out there on the desk.

I always like to fish the West Fork, he continued, and I've fished it so often that I know every snag, root or rock in all its enticing reaches. There is a melancholy advantage in this knowledge. Other fishermen will tell you that snags, roots and rocks afford ideal and unfailing lurking places for over-sized trout. They catch their finest specimens in such vantage spots. No doubt they are wholly right about it, but there is an entirely different significance for me.

I know exactly where I am going to foul a hook in the aquatic root system of some forest giant, and lose a nine-foot leader. I know precisely where, in the merriest water imaginable, I shall lodge a sinker neatly and inextricably in an eager, lurking lithic crevice and part at last with possibly seven feet of line and a favorite spinner. You see the advantage this is to me. On the West Fork I am immune to the usual disappointment, vexation and chagrin that lie in wait for your common fisherman. I have fore-knowledge of these misadventures and they neither astonish nor dismay me. And this result, I have been informed, is the true purpose of any philosophic approach. So I fish the West Fork season after season on each opening day.

*   *

If ever you have fished the West Fork you will remember the smooth greenness of the bend by the black rock. On the north side of the river, which is the only bank available at the black rock bend, there is an alder tree that is by way of being an old, fond friend of

mine. It is, perhaps, the most whimsical, adroit and
waggish alder tree in all the region, and to its topmost
twig I know every branch and contour of that tree. The
cast is a long one, a fairish one, across the fast water,
and into the foam that waltzes back of the rock, and
sometimes I make it as a champion would.

But more often my forest friend, the alder, retards or
retains the pliant silk, the 15-cent fly, the tapered
leader—and there I stand, booted and manly, a true
fisherman, peering raptly upward into the intricacies of
branch and twig and catkin. I know of no more
efficacious way of inducing a crick in the neck. And
strangely I have experienced, many the time, as I drew
near the black rock bend, a psychic conviction that the
fine old alder was waiting happily for me. That it relied
upon me to introduce something of interest and novelty
into a tree's routine day.

I have given prayer, of a sort—mused the Old Copy
Reader—underneath the old alder, and I have slipped,
slithered and stumbled away from the black rock bend
while behind me my friend, the alder, was modestly,
yet brightly bedizened, with some of the finest tackle I
ever selected. Have I any regret? Not exactly. The way
I look at it, such experiences have tended to advance
me out of the primary grades as philosopher—a
practical philosopher.

* *

And though I fish down the dear familiar reaches of
the West Fork, or up, as the case may be—for I count
it not a whit of difference, since I shall meet with the

same droll mishaps, anyway—in the due course of my progress I come to my familiar rendezvous with most lively adventure. It is the appointed place where invariably I fill my right boot to the brim with vigorous mountain water, chill and refreshing. The leap, as I always regard it, is a trifling distance, a mere absurdity for a true angler—but the slope of the rock to which I address my agility is silken with watery mosses. One slips gently, gradually down to the green chasm and almost thoughtfully, as you might phrase it, allows the right boot to drink its fill like the stag at evening. Having regained the shore with remarkable ease, there is a suitable area of sand, through which a chill seepage traces its invigorating way, where one may seat oneself to remove the boot and reflectively decant and restore to the river its rightful essence. I may say, without trespassing further on your patience—he sighed—that it is customary to fill the left boot a matter of some score yards farther on, or to fill it first, according to the direction in which the West Fork is fished.

Have you the acquaintance—inquired the Old Copy Reader—of that vegetal phenomenon popularly styled the devil's walking stick, or devil's club? These lacerations you will observe upon my hands were not received in a frolic with any bobcat, sir; they are, instead, the evidences of my valiant passage through a veritable thicket of the unique and sprightly shrub to which I make allusion. There are so many ways in which the West Fork excells all other waters that it would be tedious to enumerate them all. But I make bold to say that nowhere else does the devil's walking stick attain to such profusion, intelligence and malignancy as in that brief, sylvan traverse of the forest which an angler makes perforce when he has reached the gorge. Later on in the season there will be nettles, too, but the devil's walking stick is always to be encountered in luxuriant profusion.

*   *

Yes, I fished the West Fork like always—although one cannot seat oneself in three feet of water, however briefly, without wetting the sandwiches. A wet sandwich, eaten on a refrigerated rock, with both boots squishing, and maybe a slow rain descending mistily, while a water wren teeters at you four or five feet away and winks his silver winkings. Ah, what an experience! Indeed, yes; as has been my custom for years, I fished the fond familiar West Fork on the opening day. It did not disappoint me.

May I—asked the Old Copy Reader—have another of your cigarettes? I'm obliged to you. What? Well, as to that, and in the sufficient language of chemical analysis—of fish, a trace.

FISH, FAITH AND FULFILLMENT

You have to have faith, of course—said the Old Copyreader—but what is faith without patience? They are near cousins, I'll admit, but some patient folks I've known were merely resigned and apathetic. And some folks that appeared to have faith were so impatient that they couldn't wait, although they had to wait—and that isn't faith, as I see it.

Where—asked the Old Copyreader—are those cigarettes of yours?

I was going to tell you—he resumed—about that first steelhead, if you have a few moments to spare. I can find time for it, I guess. Yes. Yes, indeed. A steelhead is a fish and not something out of a foundry. A steelhead is something finer than a fish, but I suppose when I say this I'm getting you out of your natural depth.

*   *

When the first real rains of the winter roil the streams in the coast country the steelhead, out at sea, hear their own rivers calling. And they have to come in. You may depend on it. They have to swim above gravel again and under the cedars and firs. That is the law as it was appointed for steelheads. So we fishermen, if I may style myself by a name so honorably ancient, are almost as excited about a real steelhead rain as the steelhead are. And we have to go, too.

A southwester came up, warm and wet and windy, and the two of us went down, to the coast the next day, and up the river a few miles, and it wasn't more than gray daybreak when we bailed the boat and put into the current. The morning felt and smelled like steelhead—but there's no manner of use in my trying to explain to you. It's a matter of faith, plus experience, working on the mortal imagination. We started the motor and turned the boat upriver, and we went upriver for about half an hour. Then we beached her at the edge of the willows, with that loud rising riffle and its eddy just at nice casting distance.

"We're bound to get a steelhead today," he said to me. And I said to him, "There can't nothing stop us."

Well, first off, we caught a few trout, because they were out there, schooled-up for the voyage down to the ocean. And it began to rain again. This rain was a warm one, and gentle-like, but let a warm rain get down the back of your neck for a couple hours, and wet most of your matches, and you'd be surprised how cold it will seem. But you don't mind it. You say to yourself that this is exactly the weather for steelhead. And it is.

*   *

"Ain't she exactly the right kind of a day?" he said to me, and I said there never was a nicer one, and real pleasant. We meant it, too, although he sneezed occasionally. It didn't mean that he was catching cold, he explained to me. He was subject to spells of sneezing, seemed like, and it didn't mean nothing. Maybe three or four hours passed this way, and the trout quit striking, for the river was rising fairly fast. He slipped on the bank and went in over the top of one of his boots. But he wouldn't take her off. And while I was laughing at him, hanged if I didn't get over the top of one of mine. And I wouldn't take her off. You see, almost anything might happen to your bait out there while you were monkeying around with a wet boot. Anyway, mine wasn't so very wet.

Nothing happened. Every so often a few fish-ducks would go whisking past us. We heard an old tree give it up somewhere back in the timber. It sounded like dynamite when she fell, the hollow, dull roar of it. It wasn't raining so heavily, but it was still raining, and fir needles and alder leaves were coming down on the current.

"You notice," he said to me, "that the trout have quit striking?" Way he said it was quiet-like and persuaded, plumb persuaded. "Sure, I noticed it quite a while ago," I told him. "It probably means that a steelhead or so has come in and chased all those trout away." He fairly snorted at me. "Probably!" he said. "Probably! My goodness, what in heaven's name could it mean if it doesn't mean that!" Only that isn't exactly the way he put it.

*   *

Along about noon we made a small fire, the wood being wet, of course, and boiled us some coffee to have with our sandwiches. But we kept an eye on those rods, and once he dropped a sandwich in the mud to jump for his. It was only a big mudcat, we agreed, when he didn't catch it. And likely it was that. But we sort of grinned at one another through the rain. For it might have been, it could easily have been, a steelhead.

"Do you know," he said to me, when we were both standing beside our rods again, "I believe that was a steelhead." And I agreed with him. I'd begun to believe it myself. Though I guess it wasn't.

And so the afternoon went along, with the river still

rising, and never a fish like we wanted. We were wet to the hide then, in spite of our slickers and boots, but we didn't mind it. Only thing we thought of, was would there be time enough. It gets dark mighty early up one of those coast streams.

"What do you think?" he wanted to know. She lacked perhaps three-quarters of an hour till dusk. "It's just the time of day for it," I told him. "You're right," he said, solemn as anything.

You say that was the time that faith didn't work?— repeated the Old Copyreader truculently—you're dead wrong. She worked like nobody's business. For all of a sudden that river exploded, and both of us were busy in earnest. We caught four in perhaps twenty minutes, and we could have caught limits if we'd the time. That's faith—and fulfillment. Oh, six pounds to ten and a-half. Is there anything finer to look at than a fresh-run she-steelhead?

Cold and wet—and yet somehow warm and dry, if you know what I mean. Might I trouble you—said the Old Copyreader—for another of those cigarettes?

FISHES CALLED HARVEST TROUT

Harvest trout, these fishes are called—because they swim the Columbia river at the time of harvest, when the August afternoons are long and golden, and the distant hoarseness of a river boat is mellow as a changing leaf. It is warm on the sandbar by the wide river, and a translucency of warmth is woven above the tawny sand—but the small, straying wind from the water is vague with the promise of rain. It is mid-August, or thereabout, when these fishes swim curvingly out of a green great wave, and so to their river again, and upward in silver constancy. They have come home again. These fishes are called harvest trout.

Now on the Oregon shore, and over across in Washington, the cottonwoods are argent in the small wind that passes, and there is an hour of noon when land and river alike seem breathless and tranced, as drenched with an indolent essence that is from the veins of the sun. And the call of the river boat is softened, is changed, is tinctured as the first leaf turns in the thicket beside the deep eddy. The heron is carved in the molten shallows. O small, straying wind that passes, have you anywhere met with the rain? Here on the Oregon shore and yonder in Washington, the people come down to the water with laughter, their eyes blinded by brightness. The harvest trout are in the wide river.

*   *

Harvest trout, they are called, and they hear the whisper of remote hills and cedars when they are deep in the ocean, and so they swim landward at this time of the year—and as one creature, the multiple thousands of them, they quit the mystery of the sea for the secrecy of the river. They are of the cycle, ever recurring, and here is sea-silver that knew the same

courses, the same call, when the hill was young and the
mother, the ocean, wrought at a cliff that is gone.
Always at this time of the year, and before years were,
but always when noon is heavy with the sun, and the
countenance of the land looks to the cloudless sky for
the cloud that must one day shape there. It is then the
harvest trout enter the river. The hour will be cooler
toward evening.

So people come down to the river, with laughter, and
arrange willow wands in the sand, whereon to rest their
tackle, and the sun strikes at them from sky and water
alike—for it is August. They are fishing for fishes that
are fleet as a dream, and bright as a coin newly minted,
with the sea-silver yet on their hasty flanks and their
hearts brave with the vital strength of the sea. Harvest
trout, these fishes are called—for they enter the river at
that time of year, when the dark woman, who has all
things in her keeping, has made provision for all. Small
wind that blows over the water—have you anywhere
seen rain?

BEAUTY OF THE SHE-STEELHEAD

It cannot be possible, the planet over, to discover a
fish more distinguished for beauty—not for gaudiness
and vainglory—than the she-steelhead trout of our own
rivers when she is newly ascended from the sea; when,
in fact, as fishermen say, the sea-lice yet are on her

flanks. Do not shrink from the term—these are small and elfin parasites that attend the steelhead until the migration is well within sweet water.

*   *

The steelhead is an ancient of fishes, as are all its kin, and in form it has changed not at all since times that are recorded in stone. You are bound to reflect, when you catch one, vibrant with the sea-strength, shining with the sea-tones—and more especially if the fish is a female—that when the creative artistry, by evolution or other means, contrived this handiwork it was called good.

Among waterfowl there is one superlative bird, judged by the concepts of beauty, and this is the drake pintail duck. The colors are relatively subdued, the pattern thoughtful, and the fluency of contour a perfection of line. Other water-birds, many of them, have more of ostentation, more of exclamatory emphasis, but this bird is all that an artist might dream. And so it is, in the world under water, that the she-steelhead is without parallel.

Half of fishing is the capture of beauty, quite as the other half, if not more, is the taking of fish. How comely this fish is, in all truth; how surely and graciously molded and modeled, with silver beneath, silver that is faintly flushed with pink, and, above the median line, a darkness that partakes truly of steel— with rounded dark spots sprinkled sparingly on this field, from caudal fin to oval snout. She is such a fish as an artist might have dreamed, and yet have been

incapable of releasing from the clay. There is no least
uncouthness in the beauty of the female steelhead,
nothing to mar it, nothing left for suggestion. This
work is finished.

*   *

This is not true of her mate—a personable fellow,
but given to an evident fierceness, pugnacity, plainly
depicted in each stroke of his appearance. By contrast
he seems a fish of scant fancy, who would rely upon
strength and obstinacy rather than on stratagem and
fleetness. It is a conclusion amply born out by the
conduct of the sexes when hooked and played. The
male fights deep in the river, striving heavily, or with
bull-like rushes; the female throws her lithe, beautifully
gleaming body time and again in air. She has more of
imagination. She can and does experience terror and
despair. Any fisherman will vouch for it.

Nor is it true of the salmon, of either sex or any
species. The male steelhead is far more like these, in
appearance and disposition, than is the female,
comparatively stupid and unimaginative fishes that they
are. But she is like a species apart, and there is
apparent even in the eye itself a wit and mental
resource not bestowed on salmon. She is the
thoroughbred in every line and reaction. To be sure,
any of the trout have more of fancy than have the
salmon, but the she-steelhead is the wittiest and most
resourceful of them all. This trait is compatible,
excellently so, with her comeliness.

She is a game fish that has everything, as fishermen

say—vivacity, strength, resourcefulness, intelligence and beauty, and the last is by no means least. When men have taken her they have taken something more than a fish that is estimated in pounds and ounces. They have taken dream and desire, and they know it—even while their hands tremble at the fleshed hook—and it will be wrong of them, and sinful, if they leave her to die slowly, or cast her down in the splashed earth of the river bank. Such fish are meant for worthier treatment.

*   *

True enough, the male fish is a hero of sorts, and deserving of his mate. Then, too, commercial fishermen declare that the male steelhead is superior to the female as a table fish. But it is undeniably the fact that anglers, although they may not and do not often pause to analyze their reactions, are considerably more gratified at catching a she-steelhead than by the capture of a male fish. It is here that the appreciation of beauty enters, without prompting, even without awareness, to teach that substance is not everything—indeed, that substance is less than beauty.

A "she-one," the fishermen call her; or, it may be, a "schoolm'am." Sometimes they call her, as Fred Watson does, a "sister." But they dwell on the word, whichever it is. The world over, it is not likely there is another fish to equal the she-steelhead in beauty and wit. Such a thing were scarcely possible.

HER FIRST STEELHEAD

When I look at him today in the icebox, I'm almost sorry he didn't get away. He's like any fish you might buy at the market —only I know how strong and swift he was in the gray water, and how he broke it into a white spray.

From an account of the taking of a first steelhead on the Siletz river.

The day would be overcast and chill, with chickadees tumbling through the alders and a water-ouzel gleaning at the margin of the hasty river—a day and an eddy such as fishermen hold in affection, deriving gladness from discomfort and tasting, as though it would be wine, an intensity of eagerness and familiar mystery. You are kind to them, river flowing seaward, to lend them for an hour and a lifetime something of yourself, memorable beyond phrasing—of yourself, plunging current and meditative pool, and of the solemnly observant trees.

*   *

Cast a line into the twirling slow water, out to the fretted edge of the flow, and what is in your thought as the tip bends and recovers and the line sinks to weave in the eddy? There is mystery yonder. There is a silver strangeness of strength, unseen, that moves through the secret water, the stress and violence of the river, as birds breast the winds. There is life, swift and vibrant and eager, that on yesterday flashed through the long-crested waves of the sea, coming home to its river.

Life and strength and desire, modeled and shaped in living silver, are somewhere under the restless flow of the river. It is called steelhead.

*   *

The line swayed and drew taut, and slackened in sudden idleness, and trembled delicately, and advanced to quiver with a reflective energy. And there it paused while the swirling water made a bright arrow—paused and plunged. Steelhead. Now in a moment like to this there is only the swift central river, the hissing of silk through the current, and the captive wild vigor that, all on an instant, leaps and is seen in vibrant silver against water and rock and willow. This and the quickened pulse, and hands so tardy to do the bidding, and the current of strength that flows upward along the silk from the secret places. There is neither today nor tomorrow, nor any yesterday, but only this moment. Yet after a time, according to fortune, he is drawn forth from the river and lies shiningly on the sand and the pebbles—and a pagan prayer has been answered, yet in the answer is a tincture that has the savor of grief. So short a while ago this silver shape was mystery. And time begins again.

*   *

A first steelhead—now there is something to treasure, and to have always, so surely that many a day will come when the taste of the wind, the course of a drifting leaf, the odor of wetness on bark, or any such trivial matter, will bring that one day and its moment back again sharply, as though it were wine to the palate. It is true that they sell fishes in market, where there are bins of them, yet also it is plain that a fish such as this can never be sold nor purchased, because of a difference not readily to be told.

IV. CONFIDENCES

Commentary on the Inner Fiber of Fish,
Men, a Boy and His Mother

FISHING BESIDE STILL WATERS

When the year makes on toward summer, and the river is broad and saffron with its burden from distant ranges, you will find the crappie fisherman beside still waters, where the lowland pastures are green. It is there that he composes himself to angle, and to contemplate the gentle, placid scene about him. He angles for small fishes and unregarded, for fishes scorned by those who use the fly, for fishes derided by those who take tarpon flashingly in the south, or tuna where the western sea is blue. The lures and baits he employs are likewise lowly, and before him floats serenely the unmentionable and anathematic bobber. Regard him well, for he is pariah among the chosen of his craft. He is an addict of still-fishing. He-even-uses-worms!

And excellent it is for the crappie fisherman that he cares not a bent pin for what the elect may think or say of him. And comforting it is to reflect that he is stayed and sustained by a calm, well-nigh religious in its nature, and a philosophy which teaches only that to fish is to be richly content. For the tunas and tarpons and sword fishes—the cups of silver and gold, the portraits in the magazines—let others cast the lure. A benevolent providence has provided crappies, and arranged that he may sit him down beside still waters, to watch the ripple that widens from the cork. It is enough. In the fullness of his heart—Nordic, or Slav, or Latin, or Japanese—he knows that this suffices.

To have a crappie in your hand, what rich reward is this? A flattened moon of gold and lunar-greens, a shadowed, shining captive, with a bright, sad eye. As many another common fish the crappie is very comely. It is a rule that runs through life. Beauty is not always to the high born. There is so much of beauty in commonness. A flattened moon of gold and lunar-greens, that came whirling, wheeling upward from the saffron waters to lie among its fellows in the frayed and mended creel. A quarter of a pound of gentle excitement, a moment dowered with all that fishing may confer. The spirit of Walton broods the scene, and were it clothed with flesh again it would be first to wet a line where crappies are. For he recognized, as some of us do not, a democracy of fishes and of fishermen, and gave to the chub its chapter and to the carp his praise. Had there been crappies in England, those times he

wrote so wisely and so wittily of men and fish, be very
certain that his words had lingered to extol them.

*　　　*

The strike of the crappie is in no particular an epic
experience. No spray is thrown into the June sunshine
and no tackle comes to grief. There is not any valorous
rush nor leaping, since the fish yields readily, and even
weakly, and for its ounces is of an extraordinarily
compliant and agreeable disposition. The float dimples
the still surface of the pond, tentatively, before it
cruises away without haste. It hesitates. It pauses to
ponder. It bobs thrice. It sounds the slough with
manifest deliberation. And the crappie fisherman lifts
strongly on his rod, and brings his fish to bank—that
he may hold the moon in his hand. It is something to
have held the moon in one's hand—something
memorable. Why, sirs, the brood of Adam have been
crying for the moon since ever they knew unrest.

Fishermen who fish for crappies, and such small sport
as this, beside still waters and green pastures, bear away
with them sundry minor and unregarded fishers, in the
opinion of the elect. Yes, they carry away sundry small
fishes, in the livery of the moon—yet they have also,
item by item, the willows of the farther shore, the
mirrored fringes of the lake, the calling of quail, the
sentinel heron in the shallows, all these. And mornings,
and noons, and evenings, these also they bear away with
them, in the creels that seem to hold no captures save
crappies. And, taking it all in all, whatever may be said
of them by their betters, we believe that theirs is the

best part of angling and dare affirm it, and do not hesitate to congratulate them upon a most important and beneficial discovery. For it is not all of fishing merely to fish.

OLD ROSCOE OF SILTCOOS

In a plum-colored twilight, as we cleaned the last of the catch and gave the paunchy trophies repose in coarse, vital grasses plucked from the margin, Mr. Stebbins made this confession to an accompaniment of sadly fretful throatings, stranglings and yelpings from the mudhens in the deepening sedges. The statement was wholly voluntary and it raises, I think, sundry ethical questions as to the justification of that course it portrays. And yet Mr. Stebbins is well and long known to me as an honest man, nor did this recital, oddly enough, seem to shake my accustomed confidence.

*   *

I am a poor man who live by the labor of my two hands—said Mr. Stebbins, scraping at a scaled bronze flank—and I come of poor people that never had much of anything except happiness. Yet as you so rightly observed while we were catching these fish, I am the proprietor of an extensive and costly collection of bass plugs and lures—some of these constituting rare museum pieces, others being the latest inspiration of the tackle manufacturer. It is improbable that anywhere else, outside of a well-stocked showcase, is there a collection so complete and interesting. Your unspoken inquiry is—How can I afford it? To this I will reply with a single word, an appelative, a cognomen. Roscoe.

*   *

May I rely on your discretion?—asked Mr. Stebbins, choosing another fish—Lately I have felt that I must confide in someone. There is a quality in this strange twilight, the color of it, there is something in the squabbling of those mudhens, the grieving, that moves me powerfully to speak. Thank you. I will come directly to the point, as a plug fares when one's casting excites one with its unerring accuracy and dispatch.

Roscoe is a bass. I startle you. You regard me speculatively. But, my friend, wait until you have heard all. I say that Roscoe is a bass, yet I will tell you also that Roscoe is the grandfather of all the bass in this lake, and that this seven-pounder here, beneath my hand, would be small fry beside the ponderous paunch, the massive and intelligent head, the great shoulders and broad pectorals, the enormous caudal fin, of the incomparable Roscoe. Let us forego idle speculation as to the weight of Roscoe. I take it that no angler, fishing fairly, ever shall hoist him to the steelyard, for the courage and enterprise of Roscoe are commensurate to his phenomenal proportions.

*   *

It is Roscoe—sighed Mr. Stebbins—who brings me my bass plugs. You are silent. Is it the silence of incredulity or of awe? I repeat, it is Roscoe who has enabled me, a lake-dweller of impecunious means, to

possess that costly and remarkable collection of bass
lures which so roused your admiration and curiosity.
Roscoe has fetched these to me, item by item, season
succeeding to season, in all their varied pattern. How
time flies.

*   *

I am well repaid for my pity, as you must agree, for
pity it was that moved me to release Roscoe, seven
years ago last April, when I found him floundering
weakly about in the rushes with a MacGoogin's
Gollywoggle Supreme, perch pattern, triple ganged,
bedded to every shank in his powerful jaws. Afterwards
I named him Roscoe, as we became better acquainted,
for on this first occasion I experienced only compassion
for the old hero's plight, mixed with strong unbelief,
dubiety, reluctance to receive the veritable testimony of
my astounded eyes. No matter. I had lacked for a bass
plug. He had delivered a genuine MacGoogin into my
very hand. In gratitude and compassion I conveyed that
incredible bass to deeper water, patted the vast chill
flank with a suggestive hand, and saw him glide
majestically, heavily, preposterously into the emerald
shadows. Was it a trick of sunrays, converging where he
sank, or of an overwrought fancy? He seemed to pledge
me with a grateful eye.

*   *

And that—said Mr. Stebbins musingly—was how it
began. I suppose Roscoe is really a fish in a million or
more, but still his intelligence, his capacity for putting
two and two together, his apparent realization of an

indebtedness to my unworthy self, truly astonish me. This lake was just becoming popular then and Roscoe, in his pride of might, smashed tackle right and left. One angler would laugh at another angler, until they almost came to blows, over some incredible story of a grandfather of bass—and he, in his turn, if he continued to fish the lake, would row up to the wharf some day with his face ashen, his hands shaking—and his pet particular bass plug listed among the lost. It just came about gradual, as you might say, but shucks, it was no time at all until Roscoe and I understood one another.

*   *

Yonder by the bridge, on the upper side, where the river leaves the lake, that's his favorite place—said Mr. Stebbins.—Yes, that's where Roscoe mostly lives. When everything quieted down again I'd get into the rowboat, perhaps telling them I meant to catch a mess of crappies, and sneak off to relieve Roscoe of another bass plug. When I got to his water I'd row slowly and, first thing I knew, there would be Roscoe swimming alongside. Or sometimes, when as luck would have it I didn't hear of him being hooked, Roscoe would come to his wharf, and start jumping. Like he still does. And so the years went along. So they went along. People, just like you, have wondered where I got all my bass plugs. I never told it before.

Mr. Stebbins bedded the seven-pounder down in cool, coarse marsh-grass, and contemplated it with a detached affection. He sighed deeply again. I've even—

confessed Mr. Stebbins—sent a fisherman or two, or maybe three, to cast above the bridge, when they had plugs I wanted for my collection. I don't know why I didn't do it to you. Perhaps because all yours were duplicates.

Have I—asked Mr. Stebbins earnestly—done wrong? I am a poor man, that comes of poor people, and I value my reputation for truth and fair dealing. Roscoe, of course, is only a fish, and he isn't responsible. But what do you think about me?

OUT FROM UNDER THE SPATTERDOCK

It is a place where water weed of a delicate green, as fragile as finest lace, all but covers the dark, burnished water, although there is spatterdock also, on whose broad leaves the redwing walks with his mate. Of windless willows and dragonflies, and the smaller damsel flies, too, and of a wild vine in the cottonwood, scarlet against silver. And now and then a night heron flies without haste along the quiet watercourse, and it is startling to hear the gruff, great voice of a bullfrog. As loud, so it seems, as a tugboat yonder on the near but unseen river. And clover, with bees tumbling in it, comes down to the naked clay. It is an alone place, but not lonely.

He had spat on the worm, as one must, and his bobber floated a-tilt beyond the first spatterdock leaves. It was a place that looked as though surely some great fish must lie there in waiting, under the water weed, under the spatterdock, breathing water meditatively. For this was the secret of the dark water. The naked clay was cool to his feet, and he drew symbols in it with a great-toe. There is something in the coolness of clay, beside water, that is drawn through the sole of the foot and into the heart, as though one were a plant of some kind, and grateful to be this. But the bobber did not bob. The red-and-white bobber was motionless at its station.

*   *

It might be that he had done something amiss, and not as it should be, but he considered that the bait had spittle on it and that the hook, from shank to point, was hidden in the worm. There was nothing amiss with the pole, the line, or the bait, he must have patience. Not to look at the bait. Not for a little bit. To look might mean that just as the secret great fish swam toward the bait, eager to have it, the bait would be withdrawn. He lay on the clover, watching the bobber, and thought about flying. And he would have lifted the pole, to look at the bait, had it not been that a chipmunk came out of the willows and—not to stir— not to stir—pattered erratically almost to his shirt sleeve. When he raised his hand, at the least careful movement, the chipmunk scurried away. Someday he would make a trap for chipmunks and catch some, and build them a cage with a wheel in it. Round and round. Blurringly. Chipmunks didn't mind being tame. Chipmunks liked it. Someday.

*   *

But when he looked for the bobber, the bobber had vanished. He scarcely had turned his head, but the bobber was gone. This was a startling thing, and he exclaimed aloud. Where was the bobber? The line curved down to the dark, burnished, bobberless water. Such was his astonishment at the disappearance of the bobber that he was incapable, for a moment, of lifting the pole. The phenomenon was too strange for instant solution. And when he did grasp the pole, thinking to jerk, the impulse had not been imparted before, slowly rising through the dark water, the red-and-white bobber came gravely to the surface, and floated there as motionless as ever.

*   *

He was as taut then, as tense, as a runner crouched at the mark, and the scene and the universe centered upon the motionless bobber. The moments were interminable. Should he look at the bait? No, not yet. Should he? Not yet. In his heart were both hope and despair. Why had he watched the chipmunk? Gradually the tenseness relaxed. He had failed himself. And he sighed. But even as he resolved to look at the bait the bobber stirred slightly. Then it was motionless. And he was taut again. The bobber seemed to be thinking. Once more it bobbed and reflected. Now? Not now. Now? No, not now. The red-and-white bobber cruised thoughtfully to right and to left, and then bobbed to him politely three times, and with impressive deliberation said "Plunk!" and went under—down and

down, slanting down into mystery. He lifted the pole
and struck strongly.

*   *

The redwing and his mate flew up and away from
the spatterdock. The chipmunk, who had ventured out
again, hurried into the willow. For there was a vast
splash at the rim of the spatterdock, and its islands of
leaves were tossed, and in the dark water a swirl
formed, whose heart was a golden gleam. The strength
of the fish gladdened and dismayed him. His prayer was
a primitive prayer. And at length, gasping on the clay—
yes, safely on the clover—lay the fish that had waited
beneath the spatterdock. It was his. The beauty and
wonder of it. The strangeness. The symmetry. The
golden perfection. Wreathed with water weed.
Incomparable. It was his!

And hurrying, with his heart beating strongly, he
took up the golden, great fish and the pole, and burst
through the willows, into the open sunshine of the
field, and far away was his home, a red roof in shade
trees. He ran until he could run no longer before he
slackened pace. And when he could run again, he ran
once more. Into the shade of the lane that led to the
house, with the chickens squawking and scattering, and
up the back steps and into the kitchen, dropping the
pole on the porch. His father had come in from the
barn. His mother was baking bread. They turned to
him. "Look!" he cried. "Look! I caught him!"

*   *

His mother's eyes widened. Her eyes smiled like morning when it is sunny. His mother's mouth shaped itself to wonder. "Why, son!" she said. But his father, thrusting a broomstraw through his pipestem, laughed aloud. "It's a carp," laughed his father. "A big one, but only a carp. Son, you are quite a fisherman." The screen door slapped as his father went out to the farmyard. And so it was only a carp. Just a carp. A big one—but only a carp. His mother came to him. She said, "Hold him up, son, so your mother can see him better. Oh! Isn't he a big one! How did you ever manage to catch such a big fish? Why, he is almost as big as you are!" He shook his head then, but his eyes laughed into the blue smile of his mother's eyes. "You're fooling, mother," he said, "but he is really a big one, isn't he? And, mother, isn't he beautiful?"

His mother put her floury hands on her hips, and her head was sidewise, in that way he liked, as a bird's, and the sun made glints where her hair was fluffed at her ears, and she frowned prettily while she considered. "There never was a more beautiful fish!" declared his mother. And, stooping, she put her arms about him.

THERE ARE NO SONGS TO THE CATFISH

Once in a summer past, when they went catfishing on Sauvies, and had gone through many gates, the wild sunflowers of a meadow by the Gilbert bore each a dragonfly of trembling, beaten, shimmering bronze. And there the ash cast down its pool of shade. But they had frightened the tall heron quite away. You should have seen the dragonflies they saw that day on Sauvies by the Gilbert.

The Gilbert is a languid waterway, carved deep in Sauvies, and there are watching cattle in its meadows, with the hay to their udders, and the morning sun makes them too bright to look upon sometimes, and a dark hawk hovers the covert. There is a stillness then on Sauvies that carries laughter far, and the fallen shadow under the ash is cool—as when they came to the Gilbert to the catfishing.

It is flood water now, and Sauvies lifts its thickets and its forests from the flood, and the Gilbert is wider than any man might cast, for it is wide as the island almost, and it is lost in the flood. But the high water on Sauvies is falling, falling, and the catfish draw out of the shallows into the Gilbert again, and soon there will be catfishing there.

*   *

They fished in the shade of the ash, and the lines made silver arrows far in the current, for the tide was receding. The lines quivered. They had frightened the tall blue heron away. The lines quivered, and tautened, and twitched in the yellow water, and they drew from the Gilbert such catfish as seemed of smooth gold, for that is how it is with the catfish when the water is yellow. Captive succeeding to golden captive, the catfishes of Sauvies.

This is an employment well suited to summer, for it has little to do with haste, and the sun on the meadow brews a warm wine of the grasses and gives this to the small wind that presently is drowsy and lies down. The shouting of boats on the river, beyond the far fringe of the cottonwoods, the hoarseness, is softened and changed—it is changed, it is softened, it is one with catfishing on Sauvies. This is an employment well suited to summer.

*   *

While they fished for the paunchy small golden catfishes of Sauvies they were aware that the yellow slow flow of the Gilbert had in its keeping sundry vast sturgeon. This was an inner, a passive, excitement. Somewhere under the Gilbert, armored and thorned, a ponderous shade in the shadowy water, swims the sturgeon that nobody knows. They watched their rods by the Gilbert, the secret, and drew from its saffron leisure the astonished small fishes of gold. Still there are sturgeon on Sauvies, under the flow of the Gilbert, monstrous and meditative sturgeon.

For such fishing you need but a poor rod, and a reel quite indifferent, and hooks derided by trout, and a bucket of worms, and a long day in summer, and the rod rests on its forked twig, in the silence of Sauvies, and the thoughts of the fishermen rest on the island gladly and without form. But an artificer fashioned the trembling dragonflies of burnished bronze that rest on the ragged sunflowers of Sauvies. Who cast the dark

wheeling hawk high into heaven? For such fishing a
poor rod will serve.

*   *

Last summer a man from St. Helens, they said,
fishing the Gilbert there by the dragonfly meadow,
fishing for catfish, saw the line lengthen, the tip bend
strongly, and caught up his rod to endeavor the taming
of a great sturgeon. By the blessing of providence he
landed it there where the willows bend over the
Gilbert. That was last summer, they said.

The best place of all to break bread, and to drink
from a jug of cold water, when it is high noon and the
cattle are under the trees, and the small wind is asleep
in the pasture, is beneath the old ash on Sauvies, beside
the slow Gilbert. It is the best place of all. Yet always
they watched their lines, from the pool of shade where
they rested, for the Gilbert has sturgeon.

*   *

Some journey far to the mountains, and some must
go down to the sea, and water is water wherever you
find it, placid or broken, but others go early to Sauvies,
when the June freshet is down, to fish for catfish in the
Gilbert. There is something about it, something, that
isn't all catfishing.

There are no songs to the catfish, few chapters, and
quite nobody paints him, while some have asserted the
catfish to be as ugly as any fish of them all—but to
those that went that day to Sauvies, and so to the
Gilbert, through many gates and meadows, the catfish
is a fish of beauty and desire. For his flanks are the hue

CONFIDENCES / 67

of a gold-piece, and his shape, for all its squatness is comely, and the tug that he gives to the line is not less than the stroke of the striking tarpon. You couldn't convince them that this isn't true of the catfish of Sauvies. But there are no songs to the catfish.

When the wind woke on the island toward evening and they passed through the gates again, the cattle were all going home from the meadow, and the hawk had ceased from his hunting. And Sauvies was even more still than the warm drowsy silence of noon, and they heard a dog barking somewhere. For distance on Sauvies has authority over such sounds, until they become memorable, as though they were music. And maybe they are, when is near twilight on Sauvies.

The freshet, they say, is declining. It is summer once more. The heron returns to his station. The dragonfly to its meadow. There is an old ash by the Gilbert that casts down a broad pool of shade.

THE FISH CALLED SILVERJACK

Heart could not wish any finer fishing than fishing for silver jacks, along toward the fall of the year, where the tides move to and fro in rivers that enter the sea. There isn't a better fish, a worthier, anywhere to be found, than this juvenile salmon the English would style a "grilse." There aren't better rivers, either, wherever rivers run down to the ocean. The plumed trees march steeply upward from the river to crests that nobody climbs, and there the topmost firs and spruces stand in the sun and the sea wind, and in cloud, too. At the feet of the hills the river is threaded, and it is the highway of the salmon as it was in the beginning. In such waters you will catch the silver jacks.

* *

People will be telling you that the chinook is a fish to be desired of any tackle, and that steelheads are knightly. They will have a word for the salmon trout, that are the returning cutthroats who have been down to the sea. And you must not question the correctness of their views. But to any of us who has caught the silver jack, with the tide setting strongly, and a taste of salt in the air, of salt and of wetness, it must seem that there is no other fish so dearly like a living blade. A fine fish for his ounces. An excellent fish for his inches. A fish that was wrought to shine in the sun, above the dark and moody tides.

* *

Scarce more than the length of your forearm—or even less—but very valiant and bright, that small romanticist, of fishes. It may be that the line twitches strongly, unmistakably, for a moment or so before the fish makes away, or it will happen that he strikes the bait with a rush and a flash, for sheer joy of striking, for very eagerness of being one with the salmon run. In either case it were difficult to tell which approach is more pleasing to the angler. But when the silver jack is lifted thrice and again into the sunshine, when the reel sings and the rod bends, there can be no doubt of the

worthiness of this certain fish. Few trout resist so
brilliantly, whatever their weight, and few fish are so
comely against green fern.

You never hear a great deal about jack salmon, either
chinook or silver. Even many of those who catch them
would pretend that all jack salmon should be held in
light esteem. As to why this should be, we doubt they
could answer you. What do you ask of a fish? Is it
beauty of hue and contour? Is it courage and wit? Is it
the merit of the catch when it comes to table? It is the
sum of all these, you will say. Now as to that, the silver
jack is indeed such a sum. And a very great pity it is
that he is taken by the uncounted thousands as a fish
for small commerce, and is not permitted to ascend the
coastal streams in greater numbers for the contentment
of people who are endeavoring to escape themselves.

*   *

No, there simply isn't any finer fishing than fishing
for silver jacks when the vine maples are turning. There
are bigger fish of course, mature and dignified salmon,
but there is none more lively or of stouter heart. If they
will but be temperate in their approaches, the silver
jacks provide too that meditative, friendly and wholly
unhurried communion with the river that is as a
sovereign medicament. There is time for the heron on
his driftwood. There is time enough for the pattern and
flow of the dark water. There is time for the little-small
bird that comes to drink at the edge of the eddy. Time
enough and to spare for forgetting that yesterday was
very important—yesterday that is so far away.

What have you in your creel? Let us see. Well, in the creel are three fine fishes, of the sort that are called silver jacks. Yes, they are of that kind, beyond question. But here also is something strange beyond belief. Sir, you are an exceptional angler. It appears that you have played and landed a sunset on the lower river.

V. MEMORY

Journey Back for Steelhead and Laughter
by a Driftwood Fire

AN EXPLOIT ON OLD SLAB CREEK

They fell to talking, as fishermen will, of how long it
would be until the steelhead were running in the
coastal streams again. Those magical names of rivers.
Why, sir, to be drenched beside a stream so named, in
a cold rain and utterly without driftwood that will burn,
is a happy privilege when the steelhead are running. It
won't be long now. Over a second cup of coffee, talking
of it, you smoke another cigarette. Steelhead.

*   *

It could not be, one said, a fish too highly praised for
its courage, strength, agility and resourcefulness. You
cannot praise the steelhead beyond its true deserts.
Observe the clean, fine lines of it, that shapely contour
—which mark it as a creature exceptionally well-bred—

the smoothly modeled skull so evident of an unusual intelligence. And there are many tales of the bravery and prowess of steelhead, and each of these—well, probably—approximates the truth. It is something that cannot be claimed for the narratives of other fishes.

And then the other laughed and said that, yes, it was true enough, but he should like to tell of how the Old Master, as he is called for his incomparable skill with a bait-rod, fished Slab creek one November day for steelhead. This was before, you comprehend, they changed the name of it to Neskowin creek, as though its original christening had been uncouth. But it is still Slab creek to the Old Master and every fisherman who knew it in those earlier times. If so be you may hit it right, as fishermen phrase ideal conditions, small Slab creek is a stream to haunt your memories.

*   *

He said he would not by a single word attempt to minimize the veritable courage of the steelhead, its redoubtability, but it is true of fishermen that one who is truly of the fraternity somewhat enhances the high valor of the fish, quite as a poet is inclined to attribute all perfection to the fair object of his metrical sighings. All fishermen, in so far as fishing is concerned, quite all are poets, naturally and unconsciously. You take the Old Master, now, remembering that doubtless he has hooked and landed in his time some several thousands of fine steelheads. Should it not be considered that he knows them well, the vibrancy and power and wit? Why, certainly, it should.

Then those two, so he said, fished downstream on Slab creek, in late November, in a slow rain when every rock was shining darkly. A gloomy day, you'd call it if you do not fish, but yet the quality of the daylight was oddly bright—like tarnished silver, maybe, though that's not quite the hue. You know the kind of day.

*　*

It seemed there were few fish in Slab creek that November afternoon, in spite of everything being exactly right for them—yes, few or none. The creek was high and fast, and yet of a requisite pale cloudiness, exactly as it should have been for bait. There's this about the Old Master: until he reels in the last cast of all, the absolute last, he is as confident as when he made the first. And time and again as those two fished down Slab creek he repeated that, never say die, they surely would catch fish. For Slab creek simply could not wear that most propitious look and yet be fishless. But when the afternoon darkened to early twilight, or at the hint of it, neither of them had caught a fish nor hooked one. One riffle more, he said, the Old Master, and then they must cut across the field to their car and start for home.

*　*

One riffle more, and darkening fast, and wreaths of sea-mist drifting slowly in—that queerly smoky taste, and wet, which is not smoke. The other fellow was upstream a ways and making ready to call it a day, when he heard the Old Master shouting round the bend. And he was making, for the Old Master,

considerable tumult, since at usual times even in great
excitement he is not given to yelling. But this time he
woke the echoes very much as though he were a boy
again and fast to his first big one. The other fellow ran,
with willows whipping wetly on his face, slipping on
stones, slithering on slick clay, and when he gained the
bend and slid down to the bar with a new hole in his
pants and a ten-pound boulder hunting his heels, there
was the Old Master, thigh-deep in the swiftness of Slab
creek and fast to a big one in the white water.

*   *

"He's a moose! He's a grandpa!" the Old Master
whooped, and "Did you bring the gaff?" he shouted.
Of course he had brought the gaff. He had dropped his
own gear on the instant, but he had brought the gaff
with him. That's the first law, and the last, on such an
occasion. You may forget the baby, but you're bound to
bring the gaff.

Well, sir, it was a sight to admire, so it was, and a
fisherman would travel a long distance to witness such
consummate art matched against such resolute
intelligence and indomitable courage. It was evident to
the fisherman with the gaff, as it was to the Old
Master, that that fish not only was perhaps the
whoppingest steelhead that ever swam Slab creek, but
that the Old Master would have somehow to keep the
steelhead's nose upstream or nothing could hold him.
Out where the fish was it was white water and fast.
And nothing could save the tackle, not even the
veteran genius of the Old Master, if once that

steelhead got its snout turned with the current.
Something gives when that happens.

*   *

All this time the tip of the rod was swaying and
dipping, and whipping, and veering to left or to right,
and the strain of it was beginning to tell on the Old
Master. He'd been fast to that fish for ten minutes or
so, you got to remember, and already his craft and
endurance, under conditions as they were, had been
little short of superhuman. The other fellow stood
there, his teeth chattering, wistfully admiring and
envying the Old Master and waiting the word to dash
into the water and gaff the fish. But it seemed like that
steelhead wouldn't do anything except sulk. He knew
when he was well off, they agreed.

*   *

"Do you think you could make her?" the Old Master
panted. They both knew what he meant. Was it
possible for the other fellow to wade out to that white
water and gaff the fish where it sulked and tugged? "I'll
try anything once," said the other fellow. And out he
went, teetering, balancing, and then he sort of set
himself against the current, up to his waist in the rush
of it, and scrouged his boot heels into the gravel, and
he called back, "Now give me a tight line!"

He made just one swipe with the gaff, said this
fisherman who told the story, and he socked it into
something that darned near took the gaff out of his
hands. And the Old Master broke his leader and reeled
in. It was an old red inner tube, fast to a snag.

THE STEELHEAD IS A GENTLEMAN

The steelhead—So Tony asserted—is a gentleman and his wife is a lady. They issue with dignity from the sea, returning to the stream of their nativity, and there is neither haste nor any unseemliness in their deportment. The steelhead is a gentleman of fishes, an aristocrat born, and he comes home genteelly to his heritage.

The Garden Hole is narrow as to its eddy, and shallow to futility unless the water is up—but after a day and a night of storm the Big Nestucca was rising, sedimentary, swift, and rain-pitted. The rods twitched in their sticks as the river tugged at the silk, and gulls flew slowly over, peering. She was right for steelhead and still-fishing, the river. The river was jake.

"He's a gentleman, the steelhead is," said Tony, "and his wife is a lady, and if they were people they would be real folks, those steelhead—the kind of folks that you'd like to have for friends. And why?" asked Tony. "That's easy enough. They are brave, and they're cheerful, and they're wise, and among themselves they are courteous, too. They feed usually without haste or gluttony, and though they are just out of the sea they have sense enough to understand tackle, and to be cautious about it."

*　　*

The Garden Hole was gravely noncommittal. If there were steelhead hidden in its saffron swirlings, the eddy

gave no sign, and only the mood of the river in
half-flood played with the rod tips. Yet secret in it, all
this while, there might be silver pilgrims newly come
from ocean. Tony changed baits, that the salmon spawn
should be fresh on the hooks.

"He's particular about what he eats," said Tony.
"He's no coarse feeder like the cutthroat trout, no
blusterer like the salmon. He's a gentleman from his
snout to his tail. If there's one in the eddy right now, it
is likely there are two, for the steelhead are great fish
for companionship, even before they are mated. It
seems like they chum together, coming in from the sea.
And at this hour of the morning, if there are fish in the
Garden Hole, it's ten to one they are steelhead that
came in here yesterday, for they don't travel at night,
as the salmon do. The steelhead travel days and take
their leisure at nights and they won't feed then,
either."

*   *

The Garden Hole is a good steelhead eddy, so Tony
believes, because it is one that boils gently, welling up
from its under-currents, and yet despite this
maintaining the forward though retarded flow of the
river. Such is steelhead water, where the great game
fishes may face the current, and this tempered
somewhat, and find also such conditions as are
conducive to refreshment and a sound digestion. Swift
water is the steelhead's delight, when he chooses, for
there isn't an abler swimmer—but contemplation is
dear to him. He is a meditative, decorous gentleman

that can, on occasion, become vigorous and epochal with action.

"The weather bureau might do worse," Tony continued, flipping a match-stick into the stream, "than to study the steelhead. He is a natural-born weather forecaster, that fish is. Myself, I firmly believe he can foretell weather conditions far into the future, as the sort of water we may expect in the streams throughout the winter. I can't prove it, yet I am sure it is true. The weather bureau announces, perhaps, that we are in for a spell of sunshine—but the steelhead begins feeding. And that means rain. And the rain comes while the bureau is still of the opinion it will be sunny.

*   *

"He seldom enters a stream, coming out of the ocean where he has grown large, until what afterwards are proved to have been the most favorable water conditions are at hand. How does he know? Such matters are his life and for tens of thousands of years they have been the life of his kind. I do not believe the homing instinct is as strong in him as in the salmon, and for the reason that he is not so much the creature of blind instinct. He favors the waters of his birth, but he is to some extent an adventurer, and if he finds these unfavorable he will turn elsewhere. If conditions point to a cold, dry winter, even though there is plenty of water for the ascent, he avoids in appreciable numbers the smaller streams that were his nurseries."

A seagull, feigning indifference, as though he were only strolling along the river bank, drew boldly near to the paper of salmon spawn. Tony picked up an idle rod, whipped it lightly and the two-ounce sinker sped fairly at the thief. It touched him thumpingly between his knavish wings, and without affright, but hurriedly, the sea bird rose to flutter aside.

"We will catch him a mud-cat presently," observed Tony, "but salmon eggs are ten cents a skein. Gulls are company on the river in a rainy day, when a fellow is alone. I don't mind gulls."

*   *

The lower rod was unexcitingly agitated. "There's one now," remarked Tony, and he reeled in to remove the goggling mud-cat. The gull gulped merely once.

"I am glad," said Tony, "that the trollers cannot find the steelhead and his wife at sea. They find the salmon readily enough, but nobody knows where the steelhead have their pastures, when they are roaming the ocean. Once in a great while the trollers take a steelhead out yonder, but it is always considered to be remarkable. They must feed deep, I think, more deeply even than do the chinooks, or maybe they feed beyond the sky line far off shore. So they are safe from the trollers.

"Yes, sir, if steelheads were people, they would be folks, all right enough, and the sort you would like to have for your friends. The salmon are dull beside them, and the cutthroat trout are only tricky when you compare them with the steelhead. He's a gentleman and a scholar, and his wife she's a lady."

*   *

The slicker rustled wetly, and Tony was crouched in the slow rain beside his rod. The tip bent, relaxed sharply, bent again—and then was brightly thoughtful. The eyes of the fisherman did not leave it. Now slowly it bent, as though the strength of the current would bear the tackle away, down and down it followed the taut silk, and he rose to his feet and struck. Fifty feet down-stream, and on the instant, the yellow eddy woke to sounding foam. A great argent flank flashed and curved pliantly in the gray daylight. The river received the fish again, but the line moved hissingly through the eddy, and the steel was shaped to a vibrant arc.

"He's a big one," laughed Tony happily. "He's a ten- or twelve-pounder and it'll take all of ten minutes to get him near enough to gaff."

In point of fact, it required fifteen, for he fought like a knight-at-arms, though hopelessly betrayed. The steelhead is a gentleman. What comliness of line, what mystery were there, and stilled then. The adventure was at an end.

A DRIFTWOOD FIRE BY THE RIVER

If ever in winter you build your fire beside an eddy you fished a great while ago, you will build your fire as we did—of driftwood and memories both; the one for the comfort a bait fisherman's fire will yield him, the other for a sort of gray fragrance that drifts into your heart while the smoke gets into your eyes. If you are a bait fisherman you cannot fail of understanding this; if

you are not, perhaps this remembered couplet will aid
you to understand:

> Time goes, you say? Ah, no;
> Time stays—we go.

All proper bait fishermen are sentimentalists, and this
is why, rather than because of any optimism, they
return occasionally to rivers and eddies that now are all
save barren, though once many trout were to be had
there. And they lay their fires beside these waters,
choosing from the driftwood—since the memories
choose themselves—for the reason that in other winters
they fished there with Jim or Linn, it may have been.
When the rain falls slantingly, with a dancing of pearls
on the river, and the driftwood smoke is wet with rain,
it is gently astonishing to find how much fragrance
there is in a memory. And such an odor of this, surely
it must be as an offering unto the Lord. A sort of
acceptable frankincense and myrrh by the river.

*　　*

There the beaver had worked at the sapling alders,
the slender and leaning willows, as they toiled full
twenty years back, and the bright scars of their labor
shone in the grayness. The receding river, that a few
days ago had been high and stained with freshet, now
was clear with gem-like pallor, and its tumult had swept
the narrow beach into an unmarred neatness of tawny
sand—save where the beaver had signed it with their
tracks. And the river looked as it had looked long ago,
when the bleached driftwood was growing and green,

for the contour of the little eddy had been spared by a hundred freshets. To emerge from the adlers and willows and stand there again was like entering, by the goodness of providence, the very past itself. Time had remained there. Here where so many fires had been laid and kindled the driftwood should burn once more. With the same slow rain falling; the same gulls crying over the river.

There are not many entrances by which one may come to the past again, but every bait fisherman knows in his heart this is one of them. And while he laughs by the river, and casts into the eddy, and sets his rod on the forked twig, his is that essence of happiness which is not often given—the present tinctured by the past. The shadow across the day, he would not have it otherwise than this, is softly gentle as the mist that walks so slowly with bended head. For there were three who fished here long ago, and on this sand they had their driftwood fire. Time stays—we go. But the smoke of a driftwood fire, so the bait fishermen somehow feel, puts time to naught.

*   *

Quite nobody save other fishermen has known each fisherman to be a sentimentalist. Yet it is true that fishermen do not have an affection for rivers only because of catches they made there in other days, though they may love these rivers well. The remembered trout they took, these are the pretext, for they come again to their rivers, to some such eddy as this, when the fishing no longer repays them, and they build their driftwood fires in the winter rain, and wait with patience that is retrospection for the twitch of the line, the sharp swerve of the tip, that do not come. And some would say they are lonely, but these do not understand that this they cannot be. There is no loneliness in remembering the times that they remember.

*   *

These winter days are short, and they are shorter still when you are companioned by old days that have been. Once they were short with laughter and event, some twenty years ago, when this same eddy was thronged with trout and grayling, as now it is not, and when to leave one's rod unwatched was to invite its savage, sudden theft by some lunging steelhead—as Jess Coons lost his outfit by the highway bridge. There is but little hazard now, and for long hours only the flowing current tugs at the line. Still, it is fishing, and we do not go away, to seek another place, because the best of fishing is to fish where yesterday has been.

There was a trout—it seemed a shame to take him— for scarcely had one thought to take a trout. The most curious look of astonishment was on that fish's countenance, as though he, too, found it hard to believe; there were so few of him in all that goodly river, where once had been so many. And some while later there was a single grayling, gray as silver-plate, who came striving up from the eddy where grayling once were common. And later on, along toward midafternoon, a single heavily resisting, grieving sucker.

In the old days this catch would have been derided, and by none so blithely as by the fishermen that took it. But these are not the old times, and moreover bait fishermen do not revisit the eddy, and search about for cedar for their fire, merely for the taking of fish. It is a pilgrimage into yesterday.

* *

We are thankful for rivers, and for the memories they restore to us more surely, and fondly, than almost any other medium. And the source of all rivers, the sea that never was charted, must know that fishermen are thankful, too, to be fishermen. For the gray rain, and the sweet flow of the river, for the gull slanting by, and all the timeless persistency of the river—for the driftwood that is coaxed into flame. For entrance, by the privilege which is a fisherman's, into yesterday, when the fishing was good, before the companions were scattered.

Some rivers are better for fishing, that is true, and great catches are made there today—but only, to each of us, a very few rivers are yesterday when the driftwood is kindled beside them.

VI. SERENDIPITY

*Incidental Drama Along the Edge
of the Waters*

THE WAYS OF THE CURIOUS WATER STRIDERS

The other day, for reasons it did not divulge, a rotund green cutworm inched its slow way up the masonry of the lily pond, resolutely crossed the stony thoroughfare it there discovered, and without pausing tumbled flatly to a broad pad beneath. The pad trembled and all the gold and silver fishes fled away. It was very remarkable conduct for a corpulent cutworm, that should have been burrowing into the garden loam for the sleep that is before wings. Most remarkable.

*   *

Safe on the lily pad the cutworm rallied from its tumble, and set out to explore the cool, dark plain. To westward the unhappy larva encountered the surface of

the pool and the vast deeps of murkiness. Hastening
somewhat, on this discovery, the worm made eastward,
only to encounter the impersonal and forbidding flood
once more. And thus it was wherever the worm might
turn, to any point of the compass—since its case was
hopeless. So it fell to galloping flatly—there really is no
other term—around and around the margin of the pad,
in a very ecstacy of wormish terror. For the cutworm
did not relish the role of Crusoe. And as it galloped
anxiously, seeking the escape that could not be, a
certain one drew near.

This certain one was without fear of water, for he
himself was of the water striders, that walk on any sea,
and whose kindred—circumstances permitting—may
even be found in central ocean. His slim and sticklike
body, upborne on its great spraddling legs, rested lightly
on the pool, and the entire three-quarter inch of him
was fraught with briskness and self-approval. Thus he
glided effortlessly toward the pad and its prisoner, set
foot to the leaf himself, and crept curiously near. So
much of provender and fatness he had not seen in any
month, of all the months since April, when he had
quitted the egg. It was a sending.

*   *

With these reflections, or their equivalent, the water
strider hurled himself quite cheerfully upon the
cutworm and seized that fatness near its rounded green
posterior. Their relative weights were those of the
coyote and buffalo. At this attack the cutworm, though
without means of punitive defense, evinced an

unsuspected litheness and agility, together with monstrous strength. It reared, and writhed, and contorted itself, with bewildering rapidity. It lashed out heavily in its hurt. And at length, with a great, purposeless effort, it tore free from the grip of the predacious one and cast the water strider far into the pool—a distance of inches. But the strider fell lightly as chaff.

Thus fallen, the water insect pondered its experience, motionless on the water, dimpling the surface with the slight pressure of its feet. So much of fatness and of provender—when even gnats were but occasional. It slipped forward to the second attack, and launched itself upon the agitated green larva. But almost in the instant, even as it felt the pain of its fresh wounds, the cutworm writhed from the margin of the pad into the murky water and sank heavily. A small silver fish swept up to it as it descended, and followed it into secrecy. But the water strider could not follow, being as straw that is animated, and went about its other affairs without visible regret.

*   *

That the water striders are insatiably curious must be evident to any that has observed them. And that they are the sanitary police of the surface is also evident. The trapped insect or the spent carcass, it is all one to them—they surround it with an eagerness of appetite, and they wage ludicrous, stiff-legged conflict for the spoils. Between them and the fishes, the wild fishes, there is a truce that seldom is broken.

So it is that water striders may be plentiful in streams or lakes where fish are many, and though the fishes rise to other insects they will not rise to these. Yet there are occasions when the truce is broken, for bass have been taken with striders in their stomachs, and also trout that had dined sparingly upon that lean nervousness. Though trout may rise for other insects without occasioning excitement among the striders, there are other and infrequent times when the flash of a trout will send the insect leaping high in air. Is the temper of the trout known to the insect before ever the fish is seen?

*   *

I recall an instance that will serve to illustrate. For days we had fished the one eddy on the Siletz river, and, the water being quiet near to shore, water striders were numerous. The eddy was populous with trout, and though these often rose to the surface after the lure, and many of them were drawn from the water, striving against capture, the water striders apparently gave no more heed to the fish than was required for moving nimbly aside when one was hooked. And certainly, had the insects suited the palate of the fish, the trout would have risen for them.

In a quiet hour, when the fish had left off striking, a large, paternal water strider was loitering across the pool. Under him lifted, as a blade flashes, a playful trout. To all appearance this rise of the fish differed not at all from the rise of 50 such fish that same day, in the identical water. But the water strider was of another opinion. At the swift shimmer of that turning flank the insect left the surface with a prodigious leap, springing a full yard or more to the safety of a log, where it lingered for some moments. But when it entered the water again, it did so with every manifestation of restored confidence, rejoining its cruising fellows. And though trout flashed thereafter, the insects were undistrubed.

* *

The water where bass are hidden is a favorite water for the striders. Doubtless they maneuver carelessly above many great maws, and hungry ones, at that. Not only bass, but other surface feeding fishes such as the crappie, sunfish and chubs, lie hidden beneath them. Yet I have never witnessed the strike of any fish to be aimed at the insects, nor have I seen the striders in the least agitated by those fish which were rising in their near vicinity. And once only, in examing the stomachs of pond fishes, have I found the remains of the forbidden food. It was a bass that had dined upon them, and heartily—for its paunch was heavy with their dry, brittle bodies, to the number of several score.

A DROWSY WATER

There were thin, pearl-hued films of sunlight slanting through the pool, and these revealed, as the multitudinous mist is seen, that lesser life which so eludes the eye—a microcosmic water world dense and tenanted as any jungle, yet impalpable as vapor. The sun, the life-giver, and the water that is his mate, these two are miracle.

Hasten if it please you, to the sea, swiftness of whispering current—to the sea and forgetting, as it was in the ancient times, ever returning—go forward in haste and in laughter. Here in the arm of the meadow, bent greenly to shield it, rests the refuge of quiet and drowsy water, and thimble-berry blossoms are mirrored in its shallows. There is no haste for the pool by the alders.

*   *

Do not the trout parr have leisure and wisdom, that move through the golden water and rise for such midges as are not seen to the eye? There is peace for a long, great while in the drowsy water, peace and pretending to greatness, and play in the shallows—and after, but only after, there is the swirl and urgency of the river in spate. Long after, and long. Time enough for unreckoned tomorrow. Time enough for the sea. This is a drowsy, meditative and useful water, golden with peace.

Strange sun-tinted water, wearing tall sedges of comely verdure—a green and amber quietude drawn apart from the urgent stream, that life may increase and learn prudence—prudence and courage—before it puts all to the venture. Sea by the dunes and the headland, ocean that fails not to call and to claim them, you must call for a season. Listen. She calls to the trout parr that one day shall hear her. There is nothing of haste in the pool.

A newt drew out of the shadows, where the hillwater deepens secretly, and turned like a tired flame. And he was brown as a velvet sleeve, and the flank and belly of him quickened to warm orange, and he sprawled as monsters sprawl and swam as the monsters swim. And through the chill crystal, that yet was golden, too, the sun warmed him in his chillness as it searches the veins of leviathan—the sun, the life-giver, that is mated to the maternal stream. Mark how the craftsmanship has modeled him, broodingly infinite in its stroke, patient beyond time, into the beauty of the grotesque, the strange, forbidding charm of that which has the seeming of evil. This dullard, monstrous innocence, dull-hearted, drowsing in the sun, beneath the loitering water.

*   *

Teach us, therefore, by such an one as this, to seek for beauty wheresoever the beautiful is fugitive or hidden, for there is surpassing store of wonder, and of innocence, whereat the glance should kindle, and yet not disdain—and we have seen but dimly. Teach us the beauty we have not interpreted.

Now a caddis-fly in its infancy, when it is armored in plate of stone, cares dearly for this pool in the arm of the meadow, and here there are many such at their gleaning—and here, by grace of providence, is visible beyond ordinary the hand of the craftsman. Whence came the inspiration of this stratagem, small sluggard, so to wear plate of stone? What armorer instructed? What long ages heard the lesson given? And such provisions, so the theorist tells, have come to pass by hazard and slow trial, through times long past. It avails nothing. Here the craftsman wrought, by such a pool as this, ever so long ago. Was it an instant only? Time is our fiction. Give you fair weather, creature that was considered, when your wings are grown—fair weather and an hour of happiness.

A drowsy, sun-drenched loitering of chill hillwater whereon the whirligig beetles, each gleaming dervish of them all, dance tirelessly as being strong to their joyousness. And there the water-striders glance and dart, their footfalls shadowed on the vital ooze. The water-boatmen, that are fierce and alein to fear, go curiously about their momentary ways. Strange life, persistent and recurrent, fecund beyond imagining, and brave to dare—upward and upward from the vital ooze, the microcosm of the pool, this golden, scarcely stirred placidity, upward and outward to the hastening stream, and to the sea's self waiting yonder.

*　　*

Listen. She is calling to the trout parr. The sea is calling. But they rise for midges in the golden water where dragon-flies are born. They poise and hover in the drowsy pool. Listen. The sea is calling. But where the thimbleberry blossoms are mirrored, in the place of the pool that rests in the arm of the meadow, there is nothing of haste. Let it come to a time of spate, in a wildness of rain, on some distant tomorrow. Listen. The sea calls to them. But there is no haste in a drowsy water.

THE SEA GULL AS AN ANGLER'S COMPANION

A gull of the first year, still wearing the ashbrown dress of its juvenility, was companion to me for several hours a few days ago. I have fished in less agreeable society. These gulls of the coastal streams, some few of them, have learned that there is bounty to be had from fishermen—stray scraps of lunch, the viscera of the catch, and possibly a rough-bottom fish or two, such as sculpin or chub. Thus they are most devoted for every practical reason, but I think, too—and on observation—that in time they come to derive other satisfaction from being in the vicinage of men. It would not be strange if any of the creatures—that is to say, the wild birds and animals—should learn to know loneliness for what it is, and companionship, also. The fact that such birds as this one remain with their benefactor after their appetites are satisfied, as they do, would seem to argue that the associated idea is inclusive of more than food.

*   *

To observe a gull in the water, and reflectively, is to conclude, after all, the air is its province. It is when in air that the gull is joyous to see, displaying a perfect mastery of motion, an ease and fluency that fill one with admiration tinctured by a vague, sad enviousness. The gull in the air, and more particularly if the air be windy, is the poem that never has been written, the picture that never was painted, the song for which there cannot be music. Afoot and ashore, reduced to pedestrianism, the bird is rather awkward, progressing with an unmistakable trace of waddle, for all its buoyancy and leanness of flesh. The same physical gaucherie is remarked in the swimming gull. The alternate thrusts of the drab webbed feet propel our swimmer jerkily, as though at any moment the bird might go under by the bows—which, as you must know, is not at all to be feared, since it is impossible for the gull to submerge. The levin-like diving of the grebe, or the more deliberate submerging of ducks, are quite beyond him. Such food as gulls derive from the water must be seized on the breast of the tide or current, or at most a few inches beneath.

For a time this companion of mine, sent to shorten the long intervals between strikes, fed voraciously. Salmon eggs, fish, sandwiches and fish cleanings went down the ready maw to the total, I believe, of a weight fully equal to that of the bird. Sundry ounces of salted eggs, heavy with brine, occasioned a not unnatural thirst which the bird slaked by frequent drinking of the river water. One never thinks of a sea bird as requiring water for this purpose. I do not recall that ever I have seen a gull drink save on this and one similar occasion.

*   *

After a while the appetite of the gull became somewhat jaded, and it permitted various morsels to escape, manifesting a disposition only for what it seemed to regard as dainties. Nevertheless, it continued to play the mendicant, watching me with the brightest of eyes and tilting its head slightly at such times, in that way birds have when they anticipate largess. A certain eccentricity of conduct I may have deliberately misinterpreted, but it appeared to me that the gull meant the action for a message, and, lacking a common speech, for a sort of dumb show. A honey-hued leaf, or a splinter or driftwood, would approach with the current, and this the mariner—if it came within a yard or so—would invariably appropriate, turning it about in his mandibles, pretending that it was food, and regarding me meantime as to say: "To such extremity as this is a starving gull reduced."

I could not but be astonished at the remarkable attentiveness of the bird to all the sights and sounds around it. A flight of juncos, tossed from the gray and wind-tinted alders across the stream, brought the head alertly aside and upward that the passage of the smaller birds might be witnessed. My slightest movement appeared to have significance for the gull, but rarely that of fear. At times the swimmer reacted to sounds I could not hear, and would suffer the current to bear him downward while he listened intently. A small brown bird, of the wren kind, flew nervously back and forth across the mouth of a little dark creek, but never without being observed by the gull.

*   *

An itching of the crown, doubtless occasioned by some parasite peculiarly loyal to gulls, brought the rounded head far under water, where it was smartly cuffed and scratched by a vibrant foot—blurringly. This action, manifestly, was chicken-like. Indeed, our friend, who is called by Masefield and others the reincarnated soul of a sailor lost at sea, had in several particulars the bearing and habit of a seagoing cockerel. With his wing tips folded in most unseamanlike fashion, the starboard pointing sharply to port and the port to starboard, with his plump breast bobbing to the web strokes and with his general air of gastronomic expectancy, the bird seemed more suited to the poultry yard than to the river.

Often you hear or read of gulls that have, through whatever association of ideas, wedded themselves to the companionship of men. Keepers of lights tell such tales as this. Lonely man and—shall we not venture—lonely bird. There was a rickety, weathered little schooner that once was familiar to an Oregon port, and she possessed, or was possessed by, her own private and particular gull. Some said that the bird went to sea with the schooner. Certain it was that the gull haunted the shabby little vessel when in port, and equally certain it was that the skipper would have slain the man who harmed his pet. He would curse the gull roundly but in a warmth of friendship, and it would flutter above his head and come to rest on the galley. I knew an aged salmon-trout fisherman down the Columbia river who used to call his gulls inshore when he had caught a rough fish for them. "Here, boys!" And they would come almost from mid-river, but whether to sound or gesture I cannot tell.

*   *

For whatever value the information may have, I think I should say that this gull who was companion to me consumed three sculpins, an entire skein of salmon eggs, the viscera of a large silverside and two sandwiches. Then he languished, so to speak, and simply rode the eddy, looking fondly toward me. And that's friendship in any language.

VII. AFTERGLOW

*Advice for Scoundrels, a Sauce for a Lady,
& the Reverie of an Old Poacher*

TREATING OF THE FRYING OF TROUT

As to the best way in which trout may be cooked, I came upon the advice of Lilian Tingle not long ago, wherein she asserts that the fat must be either cooking oil or vegetable shortening, and of a depth sufficient to cover the fish. And this authority touches as well on sundry other necessities, the seasoning, the beaten egg, the sifted crumbs, the temperature of the fat and the garnishing of the dish itself. Such trouts as Miss Tingle would fry, you may be very certain, could not be other than delicate of flavor, and flawless of hue. They would be golden as ducats, and we are fain to believe the authority when she adds that, however delightful they may be when hot, "they are also good cold for a picnic."

*   *

Now, mark you, here is no disposition to decry in
least degree the method so charmingly advocated by
Lilian Tingle. It will serve very well for the frying of
trout and you may have every confidence in it. Yet I
cannot but confide to you this pertinent fact, that
nowhere in her dependable advice to housewives, whose
husbands somehow have acquired trout and merit, do I
discover the least mention of the proper sauce for such
a dish. Indeed, and wholly apart from this lack it comes
to me that I entertain quite positive notions of my own
on the cooking of trouts, and that I share these with
many fishermen who are careless of rain or foul
weather.

*   *

The proper sauce for trout, of course—the one
requisite sauce—never appears on the platter. It is finely
and inimitably blended of the wind in the cedars, the
ceaseless gurgle and gossip of the stream, the odor of
clover, perhaps—or of wet leather—the chill of a forest
twilight, and a pervasive, healthful weariness that is
itself a blessing. Such is the sauce for a dish of fried
trouts. Scarcely do I need to point out to you, Miss
Tingle, the failure of the urban kitchen to provide these
certain condiments, and gladly do I absolve you of all
fault. One must contrive to get a dinner from such
materials as are at hand.

*   *

We were four on upper Drift creek when last I
tasted trouts that were cooked as I would have them.

And Herman, the reformed barber who now practices real estate, reddened his round countenance above the battered frying pan. Of food other than trout there was little. A mere handful of coffee for the blackened lard pail. A fragment or so of stale bread. And if you looked away across the ranges, the tumbled, waiting hills, across forest and canyon and creek and river, you might perceive the general direction of the nearest grocery store, but naught else. However, there was bacon in thick strips—and he who complains of the fare while bacon is yet in the pack and trout are in the creel or the creek would grumble at the hostelries of heaven. And night came on with vast and velvet strides. A star burned over the clearing. His face was ruddy as a smith's the while he turned the fish and tended the coffee. Into the night, wandering off to perplex some distant, moody predator, to disturb the bear, perhaps, and fill him with a vain unrest, went the unified fragrance of cut-throat trout and smoking bacon grease. Thus presently we fell to, and afterwhiles knew a deep content, and spread our blankets and smoked, speaking only as the spirit moved.

*　　*

Now I say to you in all seriousness, Miss Tingle, that such are fried trouts of the best, and though you scarce would dare bring such a dish to table—what with your fame and all—that the delectability of these fish would pry St. Simeon Stylites from his pillar, and quickly enough. He would course toward the origin of that fragrance as the beagle seeks its rabbit. Mea culpa!

After all, we are but mortal. Fish that are so fried, I do
not hesitate to admit, are many a time scorched and
broken in the process. They arrive with their tails in
their mouths, and their silvern ribs projecting at
random. It may even be that blades of blackened
meadow grass adhere to them, in lieu of greenest
parsley, for the method is hasty and somewhat casual.
Hunger is a guest that will not wait, and whose
disposition is in nowise finical. But these are trout!
With the stream gurgling and gossiping, and one
enormous star burning whitely above the clearing.
These are trout!

*   *

There is yet another method, though I shrink
somewhat from the necessity of presenting it. However,
if Miss Tingle may fearlessly avow her methods to be
best and her trouts to be superior, am I then so craven
that I will play traitor to mine, and not speak out for
them? This method asks only for trout, and driftwood,
and sand, and salt and fire.

The trout should be fairly large, the length of a foot
or more, and the fire must be kindled on deep sand,
and plenished and replenished until the sand is white
with heat and there are many embers. One does not
clean the trout. For the time being one is the utter
Siwash, and glad so to be. When the fire is raked aside,
a shallow pit must be shaped in the heated sand for the
repose of the goodly trout. The sand covers them again,
the embers are replaced and for the space of a half
hour one communes with patience and philosophy. But

when the fish emerge from their fiery ordeal, a sort of culinary miracle befalls. For the skin drops readily away, the body cavity yields its contents at the flip of a finger and naught remains save the flesh and bones of the finest of fishes, cooked in his own oils. Dust your trout lightly with salt, and consider the essential benevolence of providence. How simply one may live, after all and yet how gladly. Granted that one must be hungry to find instant zest in such fare. Is it not glorious really to experience such hunger, and to have food wherewith to remedy the primal ailment? Not often enough are we truly hungered. Not often enough.

*　　*

It comes to this, Miss Tingle—that you are quite right about it, from your point of view. In the very nature of things, since trout must be fetched to town when they are taken, the methods of your school, and yours only, are best for the frying of such fish under these given circumstances. Unfortunately no means has as yet been devised for the transportation of those imponderable essences which vastly improve a trout that is cooked in the hills. To have them, one must seek them where they bide.

TREATMENT OF TROUT AFTER TAKING

It may seem cruel paradox to say as much, but none the less it needs saying that a good fisherman, an angler worthy of his recreation, will deal with each trout he has taken as though he loved this fish. Indeed, if he does not accord the captive this consideration, he must fall somewhat short of being what he seems to be, and, instead, be self-confessed as a fellow of mean fancy and small gentleness.

This concern for the fish when it has been taken from the water should, if our fisherman is entitled to his fraternal standing, apply equally to all fishes that are kept, and not especially to trout. It is the trout that is spoken of here, however, for the reason that of all fishes the trout is the bravest and most beautiful, the most sensitive, and the first to fade. One might as well break a wildflower from its stem and cast it down in the ditch as take a trout and leave it untended. Of the two offenses the second is perhaps the greater.

*   *

The livery of the trout, of any trout, must one time have required much long reflection, for such color and harmony cannot be the contrivance of chance alone. And the shaping of the trout was through successive eons of meditative wonder, until its grace and comeliness seemed good to the artisan. Now trout, as it is known to you, suit their attire to the moods of the water in which they are resident, and again to their passions—so that a trout taken from underneath an oaken root may be dark as the metal of a gunsmith, whereas his blood-brother, that rises in midstream, will be tawny with gold—but in any guise of their adaptive coloration the trout are beautiful beyond other fishes. And for their beauty, as for their liveliness and valor, fishermen take trout.

You perceive man to be yet the savage, and he must have for his own the wonder of the sunrise and the sunset, if only to despoil it. But still there is, or should be, something of gentleness and gratitude in his heart, as when in taking trout he will take them with a decent reluctance, however eager, and dispose of them according to the beauty of their flanks and contours.

*   *

It is well known to you that many fishermen, as they are styled, have little thought of the trout after it is taken, but count the taking as best of all. Their trout are slimed with mud, crusted with sand, befouled by the wash of a boat's bottom, limp and flaccid from heat and moisture combined, or dried like herring in the grocer's stall. Though it is true that fishermen are alike a greedy and covetous fellowship, animated by the eagerness for possession, he is greediest of all, most covetous, least admirable, whose eagerness defeats him by the wanton marring of his catch.

*   *

A fisherman, properly speaking, would, on the other hand, prefer a half dozen of trout at evening, with something of their beauty yet remaining, something of the wonder that was theirs when they were taken, than a full creel of quite dishonored fish. There are too many clowns at this fishing, yokels who are masquerading as sportsmen and anglers, and if they are skilled, or some of them, at capture, or if they have exceptional fortune —for it is a lottery not always agreeable to merit—still are they not proved to be proper fishermen. At best they are novices and at worst they are impious. For it is undeniable that to dishonor a gift of creation is not less than impiety, and is passively blasphemous.

There is no great urgency in this fishing, and decency suggests that there is not, though the hands may tremble. It is better not to have taken a fish, and to go home with an empty creel, than to take one for its torment while it lives, and its shame after death has relieved it. Thus a trout, or any fish, should be killed forthwith when it has been taken, as a primary duty of self-respect, and not cast aside or thrust into the basket to perish of suffocation. Nor is it well to break the necks of trout, as some fishermen do, since this mars the beauty of the fish, and, if the trout is small, and is to be cooked with the head, it mars the eventual dish itself. A sharp blow, the thrust of a knife-blade, and the trout is mercifully dispatched.

*   *

There is argument of the capacity of fishes, and more especially of trout, to experience suffering—and one will say that a trout has been taken that lately was hooked and lost. Yet, at the least, there is abundant evidence in its conduct and habit that the trout is a creature of considerable fancy and much nervous intensity, to which terror is actual, if not acute pain. While as for the theoretical absence of pain, there exists no true proof whatsoever, but on the contrary there is every reason to believe that the fishes are not exempted from suffering. The fisherman who is worthy of his catch will dispatch his fish at once, as they are taken, and, having dispatched them, he will straightaway make such disposal of them as insures the minimum loss of color and charm and utility.

It is not needful to offer suggestions, or to prescribe a method, for the temporary keeping of trout in that condition, or so nearly as is possible, in which they were taken from their element. The accusatory fact is that there is no fisherman unfamiliar with such simple method, and that ferns and grasses are abundant along the waterways, yet fishermen often practice neglect. It is not within the scope of lawful authority to refuse such fishermen their licenses to take fish, pending their penitence, conversion and reform, but certain it is that they show themselves unfit to bear the state's warrant for the capture of trout. Ethically all trout belong to fishermen that love them well, and quite as ethically is it true that fishermen who do not love the fish they take, but take them only for the excitement of the moment, to dishonor them afterward, are in point of fact merely poachers upon the riffles and pools of their betters.

*   *

Do you remember the motif line in Mark Twain's great story of "The Man That Corrupted Hadleyburg"? No matter. The line is, "You are far from being a bad man; go and reform."

POACHER OF PEEPHILL FARM

How old would you say I be?—urged the old gentleman.—That's a good one! I'm 86, that's what I am, and the reason for it is that I hunted and fished all my life. With some sailing. Yes, sir; hunted and fished all my life, and look at me now. I'm fit as a fiddle. You fish a little, and you hunt a little, and 'twon't hurt you. When you're crowding 90, you'll be like I am.

Now, hunting—that's something. I fired my first gun when I was turned seven years, and it was a flint-and-steel gun, and a good one. They never suspected. I tell you, they never suspected. He was "Squire" William Hedges that taught me, and he was a master poacher. People called him "Squire" for a joke like. Yes, sir; he took me in hand and he taught me.

'Twas on Peephill farm, in old Wiltshire, and it was land that had been in our family for 500 years. We rented from Oxford college. Oxford owned all the land thereabout. Peephill is a hill, truly enough, and from it of a fair day you can see 30 parishes. It was the hill where Cromwell had his lookouts posted.

*   *

"Squire" Hedges weren't only the champion poacher of Wiltshire—none of them ever caught him—but he was our Wiltshire champion at backsword, too. I don't believe there was a man in all England could stand up to the "Squire" with the backsword. Some call it the quarter-stave. Many a head's been broken that way.

Well, sir, the "Squire" could thump the best of them.

And he taught me poaching. "Squire" William Hedges didn't practice poaching much himself those times. He'd sort of given it up. But he came to Peephill farm when father was gone to market, and he showed me the flint-and-steel gun and how to fire her. He taught me to load and to fire her as ably as any poacher, and him master of all poachers. Then he says, says "Squire" William Hedges, "Younker," he says, "they's rabbits in Peephill cover." Well, 'twas all true enough. Peephill farm had fine cover and many a fat rabbit. So he gave me the flint-and-steel gun.

That's how I began hunting. I poached away at those rabbits in Peephill cover, when father was gone to market, and "Squire" William Hedges he furnished the powder and lead, until I became uncommonly able. And me only seven years or something. I vow I was as good a poacher as the "Squire" was. He took the rabbits and sold them, and bought more powder and lead for me. The "Squire", he'd quit poaching himself —but he was a deep one.

Later, when I was about 10, father bought me a gun with percussion caps, but all the rabbits, or just about, they were gone. Father, he couldn't make out to account for it. But now and then I got a rabbit, like the "Squire" taught me, or a hare, or maybe a pheasant. And I been hunting ever since.

*   *

And I been fishing ever since I poached pickerel and perch in Bentom creek, with the oaks all along it. Some of those pickerel would go seven pounds. The Bentom creek oaks made a great place for rooks; that's a kind of crow. We killed the young rooks in the late spring of the year and people made pies of them. A man as never has had a rook pie, he ain't really had dinner yet.

And now—said the old gentleman—I suppose I ought to tell you about being one of the few men that ever lived through a genuine wind-twister at sea. I was hand-lining for cod on a one-third share, on the schooner Eliza Jane out of Shelburne, Nova Scotia. 'Twas in Cape North harbor, with no more'n a hatful of breeze, when saw I the black streak on the water. "Cap'n," I said, "yonder's wind coming!" The skipper, he gave one look and a yell, but before we could do anything she hit us. We dove under hatches just in time, for it was a real wind-twister, and how we lived through it I don't know to this day. But the wind struck us on top, seemed like, and the Eliza Jane she went down like a cork, but she always come up like a cork, too. And when the wind-twister passed, the waves was just dancing up and down, and the day calm and sunny again.

Hunting and fishing, the whole of my life up and until the present, as I intend to keep right on hunting and fishing. Now I'll give you a couple pieces of prime smoked salmon. Where'd I put my little valise? I put it down in a sort of cubby hole, and I talked to somebody, and then I come right in and introduced myself, and I began telling you about "Squire" William Hedges. You must have seen my little valise.

The first floor, you say? No, I don't recollect leaving it there. It was hereabouts somewhere. But if you are set on it, though I know I left that valise up here and nearby, I just as soon go downstairs and look for it with you. But I left it up here somewhere.

*　　*

Well, well. Now, who would have thought it? I did leave my little valise downstairs, didn't I? I call it my little valise because it is only a mite smaller than a good-sized trunk. Like the sea-chest I took from Peephill farm all the way to Nova Scotia. You wouldn't guess what I got in it. Smoked salmon! And pork chops. Of course, there's more salmon than pork chops. The pork chops is for me. You'll find that the best smoked salmon that ever made you drink water. And she's mild, too.

Hunting and fishing the whole of my life, up and until now, and I intend to keep right on hunting and fishing. But that little valise now, the way I misplaced it, that's funny.

There's three ages, you know—said the old gentleman—first the child, then the man—and then the child again.